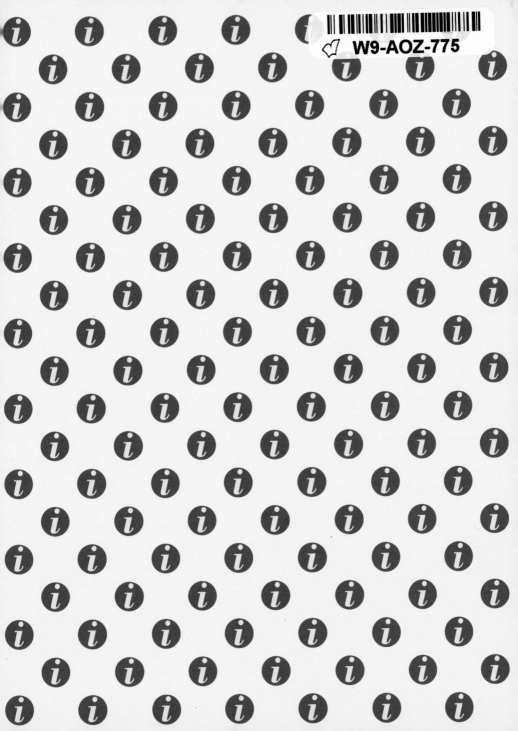

DOLLS

The new compact study guide and identifier

Valerie Jackson-Douet and
Brenda Gerwat-Clark

IDENTIFYING

i

DOLLS

The new compact study guide and identifier

Valerie Jackson-Douet and
Brenda Gerwat-Clark

CHARTWELL
BOOKS, INC.

A QUINTET BOOK

Published by Chartwell Books, Inc.
A Division of Book Sales, Inc.
114 Northfield Avenue
Edison, New Jersey 08837

This edition produced for sale in the U.S.A., its
territories and dependencies only.

ISBN 0–7858–0372–6

This book was designed and produced by
Quintet Publishing Limited
6 Blundell Street
London N7 9BH

Creative Director: Richard Dewing
Designer: James Lawrence
Editor: Lydia Darbyshire

The material in this book previously appeared in *World Guide to Dolls* by Valerie
Jackson Douet and *Dolls* by Brenda Gerwat-Clark.

Typeset in Great Britain by
Central Southern Typesetters, Eastbourne
Manufactured in Hong Kong by Regent Publishing Services Ltd
Printed in China by Leefung-Asco Printers Ltd

CONTENTS

· · · · · · · · · · · · · ·

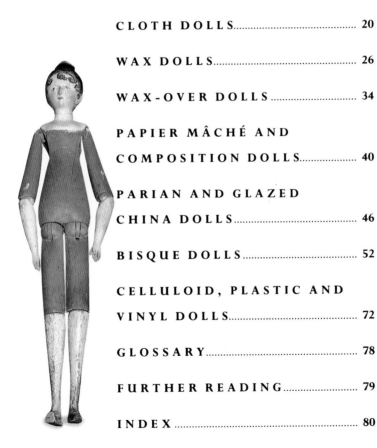

INTRODUCTION

· · · · · · · · · · · · · · · · · ·

Although dolls are now almost universally regarded as children's playthings, this has not always been so. Man has long made images in his own likeness but for religious, symbolic, votive or talismanic purposes – doll-like objects were, for instance, often placed in tombs in ancient times to represent the wives and servants of their dead master. It is not possible to say when dolls first became toys, but it is known that figures in clay, metal, ivory and bone, which were clearly made to be played with, were part of everyday life in ancient Greece and Rome. Little is known of the history of toys in the Dark Ages, but we know that toys were made in Europe in the Middle Ages and that, in the 16th century, they were taken from Europe to North America.

One of the first materials to have been used to make dolls was wood, and many originated in the thickly forested area around Nuremberg. Rag and cloth dolls are likely to have been made from the earliest times, but clay dolls were also made in the Middle Ages, and the making of small crib figures – now known as crèche dolls – and dolls to mark saints' days established the tradition of using wax dolls for secular purposes. By the 18th century, papier mâché, composition and different types of china with different glazes had joined cloth, wood and wax, and as new materials were invented – rubber, celluloid, vinyl and so on – dollmakers adapted to meet new challenges. Social changes, especially the growth of an increasingly prosperous middle class, coincided with technical advances and the development of mass-production methods both to create a market for toys of all kinds and to provide the means by which the new demand could be met.

ABOVE: A large and rather beautiful felt doll by the English maker Norah Wellings dating from the 1930s.

Today's collectors are faced with an almost bewildering selection of dolls in every conceivable material and style. As in all fields of collecting, the first rule must be to collect dolls that you like. Although dolls, in common with many

ABOVE: Glazed china heads from the late 19th century.

clothes, and some were even supplied with several complete sets, including dainty underclothes. Although dolls by the famous makers – Bru, Jumeau, Huret and so on – are rare and expensive, there were many other fine makers active at this time, and dolls by lesser known names are well worth seeking out.

Another popular group of dolls are those known, loosely, as character dolls. Many were made in Germany, and among the best known names are J.D. Kestner, Kämmer & Reinhardt, Armand Marseille and Simon & Halbig. The output of these manufacturers was so great that it is possible to find marked examples of some of these great makers. As in France, however, there were many smaller companies producing interesting and attractive dolls that will not necessarily command the premium that a famous name will add to the price.

Having decided what kind of dolls to collect, you should spend some time reading about them. Many books have been published about dolls in general and about specific periods and manufacturers, and a few of these are listed at the end of this book. These books also contain suggestions for further reading. Take every opportunity to look at illustrations of dolls by named makers. Compare the shapes of the dolls' faces and heads and the ways in which features are moulded and painted. Look at the different ways that hands are shaped and the ways in which joints are used.

other kinds of antique and collectible, appreciate in value, acquiring dolls in the hope of future profit is, at best, risky. Let your collection be guided by your personal preference and your pocket. Decide whether you are interested in a particular period or a particular material or perhaps the dolls produced by the makers of a single country. Doll are generally classified by the material used for the head. Thus, a doll described as composition will have a composition head but may or may not have composition limbs or body, and a doll described as bisque will have a bisque head but may have a leather or cloth body and limbs of another material.

Some of the most beautiful dolls ever made were the bisque fashion dolls or Parisiennes, produced in France in the latter half of the 19th century. Not only were these dolls delicately modelled and painted, many had the most exquisite

Study the ways the ears and mouth are modelled and the ways in which the hair is applied.

Next, visit as many museums and exhibitions as you can. Go to doll fairs and attend lectures. Join a doll club so that you can talk to fellow collectors and exchange information with like-minded enthusiasts. The next stage is to establish a rapport with a few dealers. In effect, this means becoming a valued customer, which involves buying – and this is why you must do some homework before you part with any money. If you are lucky, a dealer may allow you to handle dolls. Learn where to look for marks. These can be incised, stamped or in relief. If they are on the back of the head (often under the wig), they are a fairly reliable indication of origin. Marks on bodies are not always trustworthy, because an old body could easily have been attached to a reproduction head. Marks on clothing are equally un-reliable – old clothes can easily be put on a modern doll. Do not forget, however, that many fine dolls are completely un-marked. Many early dolls by the Alexander Doll Co. were identified only by paper labels fastened to the dolls' wrists or by labels stitched into the dolls' clothes.

Dolls may be damaged or they may have been mended so well that the repair is scarcely visible. This is something that a collector must appreciate. Look for cracks. If possible, undress any doll you intend to

ABOVE: The German manufacturer Simon & Halbig made dolls' heads for many other doll-makers, including Kämmer & Reinhardt.

buy. If the clothing is stitched on in such a way that it cannot be removed, it may be hiding a badly damaged or fake body. Check that all the limbs are of the same type and that one has not been replaced. Look for chipped ears or missing fingers and toes.

It is difficult to recognize a good fake. Even cloth dolls are being reproduced, as well as bisque, china, wooden and wax dolls. Look out for nylon hair, new white kid bodies, clothes made of synthetic fabrics and machine stitches. The sewing machine was invented in 1829, but it was not widely used until the latter half of the 19th century. Even then, clothes were often stitched by hand, and the stitches range from minute, finely worked stitches made with a fine needle to large running stitches.

Look for signs of age, the indications of wear and tear, on the doll as well as on the clothing. Papier mâché and composition dolls tend to wear at the joints. Very white plaster in the corners of the eyes of a bisque head may mean that the eyes have been replaced. Remember, too, that the price of a damaged doll may reflect its imperfections, and if you really like what you see, buy it – you may never have another opportunity.

Auctions are probably the best place to buy, but they are more suitable for experienced and knowledgeable collectors. Attend the viewing and look at any dolls that interest you as closely as you can. When you attend the auction, fix a maximum price and do not go above it, bearing in mind that buyer's premium and VAT will add to the hammer cost. Do not let yourself be carried away in the excitement of the bidding.

Doll fairs also provide good opportunities for buying, and you may also sometimes find dolls at a general antiques fair. If you are thinking of collecting modern dolls, you can probably do no better than to attend a fund-raising event or car-boot sale. Toys and dolls are always to be found among the unwanted Christmas presents and other white elephants.

Once you have started to acquire dolls you will have to give serious consideration to how you are going to store and display them. This will partly depend on the material, although no doll should ever be kept where it is exposed to direct sunlight.

If wooden dolls are your particular interest, you will have to pay special attention to humidity levels, because wood expands when it absorbs moisture and contracts when it is dry, which can lead to cracking. Many wooden dolls are covered with gesso and then painted and varnished. Do not wash wooden dolls unless it is absolutely necessary, and then only after first using neutral soap on a clean, soft cloth on an inconspicuous part. If the paint or varnish begins to lift, stop immediately, and never soak a wooden doll. Inspect dolls regularly for any sign of worm and, if necessary, seek expert advice about treatment.

ABOVE: A German peg-jointed Grödnertal doll that was made c.1815.

Wax is an excellent modelling material, and it gives dolls a uniquely smooth, translucent look. It is, however, easily damaged. The gentle warmth of a room is unlikely to harm wax, but hot sun or any other direct source of heat can do untold harm. Strong light will also cause the delicate colours to fade. Cold cream on a soft, clean cloth, wiped gently over the doll's face is sometimes recommended for removing superficial grime. Test this on part of the body that will not be visible, such as under the hair, before embarking on the face, and avoid the painted features. Do not use water at all. Wax dolls should never be wrapped in plastic bags, because the resulting condensation will affect the wax. Acid-free tissue paper or fine pure cotton are the safest materials.

Papier mâché and composition dolls bring different types of problems. Most have been given a top coat of varnish, and

ABOVE: A doll with a papier mâché head, wooden arms and a cloth body. It was made by the Dutch doll-maker Spijk Mijnssen in 1800.

this cannot be cleaned with water. Caroline Goodfellow suggests rubbing soft white bread over the surface to lift surface dirt. It is also possible to use a liquid cleaning product, whipped into a foam. Use the foam only, testing an inconspicuous area first, and apply the foam with a clean, soft cloth. Check that the colour is not "lifting", and use a different section of the cloth each time you apply a little more foam. Insect infestation can be a problem with these materials, and the dolls must be inspected regularly and stored with an insecticide. The faces of these dolls are often damaged – noses are frequently chipped and small areas rubbed. Unfortunately little can be done, and it is almost impossible to match the original surface accurately. Some collectors have successfully used plastic wood to repair small chips, but remember that the repair may

ABOVE: A German wax doll made c.1880 wearing its original clothing and with its original hair.

mean that the doll is worth less than it was in its damaged state.

Glazed china, Parian and bisque dolls should never be scrubbed with harsh abrasives or detergents. If the colour has been added as an on-glaze after the firing of the main transparent glaze, hard rubbing will easily cause the colour to disappear. If the colour has been applied as an underglaze, it will be protected – but if you have a dishwasher, you will know that even protective glazes can be worn away. Use pure soap, whipped to a foam, and, testing in an inconspicuous area, apply a little foam with a soft, clean cloth or cottonwool swabs. Handle these delicate and fragile dolls carefully at all times, and lay them on a padded surface before you begin work. Store them away from strong light and in places where they will not be subject to sudden changes in temperature, and if possible keep them in a glass case where they cannot be accidentally knocked over.

The early forms of celluloid should be treated as carefully as bisque and china. Although they were heralded as unbreakable and everlasting, they have not worn well, and the dolls are as fragile and as easily damaged as porcelain. Hard plastic and vinyl can be cleaned with water and a mild detergent, but always work gently. Avoid soaking the doll and never immerse a doll completely in water – if water seeps into the body it could cause mould or cause damage to joint fixing. Vinyl is sometimes stained by mould, which can be removed with a commercial preparation. Test a small area before embarking on the whole doll. A modern hazard is the ink from ball-point pens, which can badly stain vinyl. Use methylated spirits on a clean, soft cloth and work from the outside of the stain inwards, changing the cloth as it becomes stained. Do not use bleach, acetone or ammonia.

There is little point in acquiring a collection of beautiful dolls if you intend to store them away in a box. To look their best, dolls need space, and if you have only a few, invest in a glass-fronted cabinet – carefully positioned away from your central heating radiators and direct sunlight. Use special stands to support the dolls and keep them upright. Check them regularly for insect damage. And above all, enjoy looking at them.

LEFT: An unmarked French fashion doll that was made c.1870. It may be by Jumeau.

WOODEN DOLLS
· ·

THURINGIAN TURNED DOLLS

DATE: **18th century** NATIONALITY: **German** MAKER: **Not known**
HEIGHT: **23cm (9in)**

These three nursing dolls, in painted, turned wood, have movable arms. When the string is pulled the arms move up and down, rocking the baby. The doll on the left, in the blue dress, is a copy of an old Sonneberg design, but the other two are original and probably come from Viechtau, south of Sonneberg.

The skittle shape is made by turning the dolls on a lathe, a technique used also for the smaller dolls that were often included in the boxed sets of wooden toys that were available from early in the 18th century. These included farms, hunting scenes, parks, fairs and arks, complete with sets of animals, all the pieces of which fitted neatly into a special box. The same shape is seen in the stiff bodies of 17th- and 18th-century English wooden dolls.

GRÖDNERTAL DOLL

DATE: *c.*1810 NATIONALITY: **German** MAKER: **Not known**
HEIGHT: **41cm (16in)**

The skittle shape was overtaken in popularity by the wooden, jointed dolls made in the Groden Valley region of south Germany. Ball and socket joints had previously been used in artists' lay figures, but they were only gradually used in dolls. Such dolls often have pegged joints – that is, a wooden pin holds the top of the limb in position in a groove in the base (hips) or sides (shoulders) of the body. The head of this doll is in the traditional early style, with neat, painted features. The ears are carved, and when this type of doll was dressed as a woman, earrings were often added. The two shades of hair colour and curls framing the face are typical, and the carved comb, which was usually painted yellow, has led to these dolls being named "tuck comb dolls" by collectors. Grödnertal dolls range in size from 15cm (6in) to more than 61cm (24in), and they were made in much the same style for more than 50 years, so it is not always easy to date them accurately.

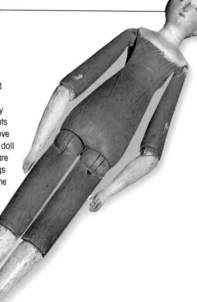

MAN DOLL

DATE: **1725–50** NATIONALITY: **probably Dutch** MAKER: **Not known**
HEIGHT: **42cm (16½in)**

This rare 18th-century doll is dressed *à la francais,* which would have been appropriate for a man of high social standing of this period. The broad cuffs, the cravat, the wide-skirted and waisted jacket, the long waistcoat and the tricorn hat are typical of the time. The doll's head, forearms, hands and lower legs are made of wood, coated with gesso. The body, upper arms and upper legs are of stuffed fabric. The features are painted, and the hair is real.

Lord Clapham, the famous early 18th-century doll that, with Lady Clapham, is housed in the Victoria & Albert Museum, London, has a similar red coat.

FRENCH DOLL

DATE: **18th century** NATIONALITY: **French** MAKER: **Not known**
HEIGHT: **84cm (33in)**

This elegantly dressed doll is part of the Galéa Collection in the Musée National de Monaco. The silk dress, which is decorated with blue flowers, is in the *sacque* or sack fashion, a comfortable style with small box pleats at the back falling from the neck and merging into the folds of the gown below the shoulders. The three-quarter length sleeves are trimmed with a deep frill of lace. Dresses in this style may be seen in the paintings of Jean-Antoine Watteau (1684–1721).

The doll's face is beautifully carved, and even the eyelids have been carefully and delicately moulded. The face and neck were coated with gesso before being painted. The hands, too, are finely shaped and finished. The doll has no legs but rests on a cone-shaped support.

ENGLISH STITCHED - EYEBROW DOLL

DATE: **1740s** NATIONALITY: **English** MAKER: **Not known**
HEIGHT: **51cm (20in)**

Under the rather round forehead, the features of this doll are well painted, and there are dark glass eyes, with stitch-like eyebrows and eyelashes. There are earrings in the delicately carved ears.

The doll's hair is swept back under a "pinner", a lace-trimmed cap, and the low neck of the dress is filled with a "tucker" for modesty, the lace of which matches that of the cap. The dress has a pointed stomacher over a full skirt, and the lace-edged sleeves of the chemise can be seen under the loose, three-quarter length sleeves of the overdress. The skirt is open at the front, revealing a quilted petticoat, and under the skirt the doll has long blue stockings and slippers with white leather soles. There are leather mittens on the carved wooden hands.

ENGLISH GIRL DOLL

DATE: **mid-18th century** NATIONALITY: **English** MAKER: **Not known**
HEIGHT: **30cm (12in)**

This doll, which is in excellent condition, is typical of English-made dolls of the mid-18th century. The face has been painted with gesso before the features were added and the whole given a coat of varnish. The eyes are dark glass, and they are surrounded by the "stitched" eyebrows and upper lashes that may be seen above. The hair is nailed in place, and the doll has no feet, although the legs are jointed at the hip. The arms and hands are of kid leather.

The clothes, which are original to the doll, are finely sewn with tiny hems and tucks, and there is also a working dress of blue and white gingham.

SCOTTISH DOLL

DATE: **mid-18th century** NATIONALITY: **Scottish** MAKER: **Not known**
HEIGHT: **51cm (20in)**

The doll's gown has leading strings hanging down the back. These do not necessarily mean that the doll was intended to represent a child, for leading strings were worn on the dresses of all dependant women in this period. The green silk dress is laced at the back, and the full skirt covers a quilted pink silk petticoat. The cap is also quilted.

The doll has rather broad shoulders and hips and an elegantly narrow waist, in the fashion of the day. The upper arms, which are silk, are attached to the forearms with wire, and the wooden legs are peg-jointed at the hips and knees.

ENGLISH CHILD DOLL

DATE: *c*.1800 NATIONALITY: **English** MAKER: **Not known**
HEIGHT: **48cm (19in)**

Although this is superficially similar to the English doll illustrated on page 14, it is not as finely made. The body is more child-like, and the long arms stretch from the shoulder, with no attempt to define the elbow or wrist joints. The high-waisted cotton smock is in the Regency style, which would have been worn at the time of the Napoleonic Wars. Beneath the smock is an older style bodice and linen slip, which suggest that the doll was re-dressed after it was originally made. The blond lambswool ringlets are trimmed with a blue ribbon, and the ringlets are stitched to a calico cap that has been nailed to the doll's head. The doll also has a green bonnet, which is not shown.

FRENCH WOODEN DOLL

DATE: *c.*1810 NATIONALITY: **probably French**
MAKER: **Not known** HEIGHT: **77cm (30½in)**

This large doll, which was presented to the Musée des Arts Décoratifs in Paris in 1909, is in marked contrast to the almost contemporary English doll illustrated on page 15. It has articulated ball and socket joints, and there are hooks on the knees to keep them straight. The hair and face have been painted on a gesso ground, and the features have been delicately carved. The doll is thought to have been made in France, but the hair is painted in the style of early German dolls. The clothes are copies of the originals, which were in such poor condition that they were unusable.

QUEEN ANNE DOLL

DATE: *c.*1850 NATIONALITY: **English** MAKER: **Not known**
HEIGHT: **Not known**

Although they are known as Queen Anne type, dolls such as this were made both before and after that queen's reign (1702–14). They are widely associated with Britain, but the style is also found in America, probably taken there by early settlers. The body was turned on a lathe, but the heads were carved by hand. The head of the doll illustrated here has a coat of gesso, black pupil-less enamel eyes, small painted lips and highly rouged cheeks. The wooden limbs are jointed, with the forearms and lower legs painted white, with green painted boots. The hair is real.

PEG WOODEN DOLL

DATE: *c.1870* NATIONALITY: German MAKER: Not known
HEIGHT: 55cm (22in)

The so-called peg wooden or "Dutch" dolls were not, in fact, from the Netherlands. It has been suggested that the word Dutch was a corruption of "Deutsch" for German, but the style actually originated in Austria. It is possible that they are called Dutch dolls because they were assembled in the Netherlands from where they were exported to Britain.

This is a relatively late example of the style. It has a fully jointed body but is less shapely than, say, the earlier Grödnertal dolls and even the early turned dolls (see page 12). The features are rather crudely painted on the awkward, skittle-shaped face. The mouth and cheeks are roughly painted, and the hands and feet are little more than knobs. The hair is a plain black cap with no curls around the forehead and temples, although some attempt has been made to add a few extra curls on top of the head.

The doll has been finely dressed in clothes that seem to be in the fashion of the late 19th century, but they are not original. It is a fairly tall doll, which gives scope for the use of more ornate materials and trimmings than are suitable on a smaller one.

JOEL ELLIS DOLL

DATE: *c.1873* NATIONALITY: American MAKER: Vermont Novelty Co.
HEIGHT: 30cm (12in)

This rare doll is not especially beautiful, but it is interesting. It has a wooden head and body and metal hands and feet, which are encased in boots. There are mortise and tenon joints at the neck, shoulders, elbows, hips and knees.

The Vermont Novelty Co., of Springfield, Vermont, USA, made wooden dolls in a style patented by Joel Addison Hartley Ellis (1858–1925), also of Springfield, who was one of the earliest US doll-makers. The early firm of Ellis, Britton & Eaton was succeeded by the Vermont Novelty Co., makers of unusual all-wooden, articulated dolls such as this one, which are known as Joel Ellis dolls. The head and body were turned in one piece, and because the dolls resembled German artists' lay models, they are sometimes also known as manikins. They were made in three sizes, 30, 38 and 46cm (12, 15 and 18in). The heads were pressure moulded and hand painted and had either dark or fair hair. These dolls are extremely rare and very expensive, and they are not generally found outside the United States.

BRISTLE DOLLS

DATE: **mid-19th century** NATIONALITY: **German** MAKER: **Not known** HEIGHT: **6cm (2½in)**

Bristle dolls were among the first attempts to make dolls that moved, and they were widely exported from Sonneberg from 1780 onwards. Also called dancing dolls or piano dolls, the toys had small bodies that were supported on four bristles. When they were stood on a piano or drum, the articulated legs "danced" about as the bristles vibrated when the instrument was played. The dolls' bodies were sometimes made of moulded dough or composition. These simple toys were known in Germany as *Docken*, and in addition to the

dancing *Docken*, there were clapping *Docken*, which had hollow, turned bodies filled with peas or grain, which sounded like rattles or made a "clapping" sound when shaken, and pulling *Docken*, which, like the turned dolls illustrated on page 12, had a piece of string attached to them that, when pulled, caused the dolls' arms to move up and down.

SCHOENHUT DOLL

DATE: **c.1914** NATIONALITY: **American** MAKER: **A. Schoenhut & Co.**
HEIGHT: **41cm (16in)**

This attractive girl doll, with its eager expression, is an example of the work of the Philadelphia company A. Schoenhut & Co. Albert Schoenhut, the descendant of German wood-carvers, emigrated to the United States when he was 17 years old. Within five years, by 1872, he had founded his own company. Between 1911 and 1926 the company produced All-Wood Perfection Art Dolls, which were fully jointed at the neck, shoulders and elbows, wrists, hips, knees and ankles. The joints were held in place by "patent steel spring hinges having double spring tensions and swivel connections", which made it possible for the doll to be moved easily yet to hold its position. Many of these dolls have survived, even though the surface paint has been lost.

The heads were modelled from solid basswood, carved by the Italian woodworker Graziano, who was one of the best known sculptors of the time. The dolls had either carved hair or mohair wigs (human hair was never used), and they were painted with natural oil-based colours, so that they could be cleaned. Toy shops sold separate outfits for them.

MODERN STUMP DOLLS

DATE: **late 20th century** NATIONALITY: **English** MAKER: **Robin and Nell Dale** HEIGHT: **20cm (8in)**

These modern dolls echo the lines of the early turned dolls. They were made by Robin and Nell Dale, members of the British Toy-makers Guild, who work in the north of England. The Dales make a wide range of turned and hand-painted wooden figures and chess sets, in addition to the butcher, policeman, chef and farmer's wife seen here. The dolls are more sophisticated and more brightly coloured than their 18th-century counterparts, which were known as stump dolls because they were made from stumps of wood.

ALMUT AUGUSTINE DOLL

DATE: **1990s** NATIONALITY: **German** MAKER: **Almut Augustine**
HEIGHT: **approximately 36cm (14in)**

At the opposite end of the scale to the stump dolls is this intensely naturalistic doll made by the German doll-maker Almut Augustine, who died in 1992. She trained as a kindergarten teacher and began to make dolls when she was 17. Some of her dolls have soft bodies, but this is made entirely of lime wood, which came from trees cut down near her home in Nuremberg. The hair used on this doll is from a neighbour's child.

CLOTH DOLLS

. . . .

ART FABRIC MILLS DOLL

DATE: *c.*1900   NATIONALITY: **American**   MAKER: **Art Fabric Mills**
MARKS: **Art Fabric Mills/New York/Patented Feb 13 1900**
HEIGHT: **63.5cm (25in)**

The Art Fabric Mills of New York produced several cloth dolls from 1899 until about 1910. The date on the doll's foot indicates the date of the design patent, not the date of manufacture. This doll still has the remains of the printed hair and hair ribbon and facial features. The body is stuffed, and hands are simple, rather primitive stumps. The stockings are printed red, and the black printed boots are laced. The company also made life-sized dolls, which had gusseted feet so that they could stand upright.

MARTHA CHASE DOLL

DATE: **early 20th century**   NATIONALITY: **American**
MAKER: **Martha J. Chase**   HEIGHT: **51cm (20in)**

Martha Jenks Chase (1880–1925) of Pawtucket, Rhode Island, began making soft, unbreakable, washable dolls for her family and friends, but they were so successful that they were soon produced commercially. By 1922 19 different models were being produced, and after her death in 1925 the firm was run by her husband and son for many years.

Although the dolls tend to look rather crude, they have a certain realistic charm and vigour. The dolls' heads were made of stockinet stretched over a mask, then sized and painted with oil-based paints. Ears and thumbs were applied separately, and the eyes and hair (which was usually fair) were painted. Dolls made before 1920 had joints at shoulders, hips, elbows and knees. This doll has rigid arms, but the cloth legs are hinged at the knee. It is not marked (although the mark may well have worn off or been washed off), and it has been rather badly overpainted at some stage in its history.

Chase also made dolls representing characters from Charles Dickens's novels and from Lewis Carroll's *Alice in Wonderland*, and many of the dolls representing babies and young children were used in hospitals for training nurses.

STEIFF DOLL

DATE: *c.*1910 NATIONALITY: **German** MAKER: **Steiff** HEIGHT: **38cm (15in)**

The firm of Margarete Steiff, at Giengen near Wurtemberg, is best known for its wonderful teddy bears, but from 1893 it also made dolls, which were designed by Margarete Steiff herself. The dolls are instantly recognizable from the seam that runs down the centre of the face. The company was founded in 1877 as a manufacturer of ready-made felt clothing, and the early dolls have felt masks, to which button eyes are stitched. The dolls are not especially attractive, but Steiff's aim was to make them realistic. They are sturdily made and are able to stand upright. This doll has an open mouth and plaited wool hair. Later dolls were made of plush or velvet, but they still have the seam down the centre of the face. From 1905 most Steiff dolls have a metal button in the left ear, *Knopf im Ohr,* which serves as an easy means of identification, but the dolls are also characterized by the disproportionately large feet. A range of character dolls produced by the firm after 1911 was largely designed by the painter and designer Albert Schlopsnies, whose own toy-making company was acquired by Bing in 1921.

DEAN'S TRU-TO-LIFE DOLL

DATE: *c.*1913 NATIONALITY: **English** MAKER: **Dean's Rag Book Co.**
HEIGHT: **33cm (13in)**

Dean & Son Ltd of London was founded in the 1840s, and under the management of Samuel Dean, its subsidiary, Dean's Rag Book Co. Ltd, began to make rag cut-out dolls from 1903. The Tru-to-Life dolls, which were registered *c.*1917, could be bought in sheet form or ready-made from the factory, where they were pressed onto a stiff backing to produce a moulded face. This technique allowed more realistic rag dolls to be made. Dean's Rag Book Co. produced many different designs in the Tru-to-Life series, both dressed and undressed, when they wore the lace-trimmed chemise and pants shown here. Another innovation of the series was the fact that the dolls' feet had soles, clearly visible on this doll, that enabled them to stand upright. Dean's trademark was printed on the feet. (See also page 25.)

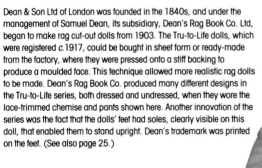

KÄTHE KRUSE DOLLS

DATE: **1920–30** NATIONALITY: **German** MAKER: **Käthe Kruse**
MARKS: **right-hand doll signed and *13449***
HEIGHT: **left-hand doll 43cm (17in); right-hand doll 53cm (21in)**

Käthe Kruse (1883–1968), who was born in Breslau, Silesia, was an artist who used her own children as models for her very realistic dolls. The first dolls were made for her own family, and she started to work to commission from about 1910. The dolls' heads were made of painted, stiffened muslin, moulded in two halves, which were joined together and filled with stuffing. The bodies were made of layers of cotton, wound around a metal armature.

The dolls illustrated here, with their painted, realistic faces, are characteristic of her work. The cloth hands have separate thumbs but only suggestions of fingers. The doll on the left has painted hair, which is typical of the dolls produced between 1910 and 1929. This doll's head is believed to have been based on an original by the Flemish sculptor François Duquesnoy (c.1597–1643). The doll on the right has a wig and was probably made somewhat later.

KÄTHE KRUSE DOLL

DATE: **c.1925** NATIONALITY: **German**
MAKER: **Käthe Kruse** HEIGHT: **43cm (17in)**

The rather solemn, wistful expressions on the faces of early Käthe Kruse dolls are said to have been intended to reflect the sadness of life in World War I. This doll, which is wearing Dutch national costume, complete with clogs and cap, has painted hair and features. The thumb has been added to the hand, which has only stitched fingers, and there are joints at the shoulders and hips. The dolls were advertised as being: "Lifelike reproductions, soft, durable, washable, made entirely by hand of impregnated nettle-cloth." Early Käthe Kruse dolls were sometimes weighted with sand to make them feel more lifelike.

LENCI DOLL

DATE: *c.*1920 NATIONALITY: Italian MAKER: Lenci
HEIGHT: 30cm (12in)

Lenci is the trade name adopted by Enrico Scavini when he started to produce pressed-felt dolls in the early 1920s. Early Lenci dolls were mostly ethnic, character and little girl dolls, and they were all designed by Elena Scavini, Enrico's wife, and her brother. As the firm grew larger, well-known artists designed the wide range of dolls that can be found.

This Lenci doll has curly hair, which has been attached to the head in strips, and painted, sideways-glancing eyes. The mouth is closed, and the doll's body is of stuffed felt.

The company still exists and continues to produce good quality felt dolls.

LENCI DOLL

DATE: 1925 NATIONALITY: Italian MAKER: Lenci
MARKS: 5 on sole of foot HEIGHT: 46cm (18in)

At first Lenci dolls had moulded felt bodies, which were not stuffed, but these were gradually superseded by cotton torsos and felt shoulders. This Lenci doll, known as the Tennis Player, was one of the range of dolls sold by Liberty of London, and it was bought there in 1925. It has brown, sideways-glancing eyes and is wearing the original clothes and shoes. Some Lenci dolls have a paper label, some a metal button and others, such as this one, have a mark stamped on the sole of the foot. Most are unmarked, however, and they can easily be confused with similar dolls.

L U C Y

DATE: **1930s** NATIONALITY: **English** MAKER: **Norah Wellings**
HEIGHT: **80cm (31½in)**

This large doll, which is known as Lucy, was made by Norah Wellings.
It has a pressed felt face with painted features, including the blue eyes,
and a closed mouth. The felt body is jointed, and the hands are unusual
in having separate fingers. The wig is mohair, and the doll is wearing
its original clothes.

Norah Wellings dolls were made in a wide range of sizes – from
18cm (7in) to 90cm (35½in) – but they all have swivel heads, and
some, but by no means all, are fully jointed. (See also below and
page 25.)

C H A D   V A L L E Y   D O L L

DATE: *c*.**1935** NATIONALITY: **English**
MAKER: **Chad Valley Co. Ltd**
MARKS: **Hygienic/Made in England/Chad Valley Co.**
HEIGHT: **27cm (10½in)**

Chad Valley Co. Ltd, a Birmingham-based company,
was founded in 1823, and it specialized in
promotional dolls and toys, including those based
on characters from films and comic strips, including
Bonzo, a bull terrier pup, immortalized by the *Daily
Sketch* newspaper. In the 1920s the company
produced Mabel Lucy Atwell dolls and a series based
on Snow White and the Seven Dwarfs.

The sailor, whose hat band bears the name "HMS
Furious", was designed by Norah Wellings (see page
25), and it was made in dark blue velvet. Such sailor
dolls were sold as souvenirs on ocean-going liners.

DEAN'S RAG BOOK DOLL

DATE: *c.*1930 NATIONALITY: **English** MAKER: **Dean's Rag Book Co.**
HEIGHT: **1m (39in)**

This is a fine example of one of the large dolls made by Dean's. From its origins as producers of cut-out dolls and rag books, it expanded to make more sophisticated toys and dolls, many of which were jointed, had glass eyes and were free-standing. It also made costumes for its dolls, and produced a range of dolls dressed in the latest fashions, many of which more closely resemble boudoir dolls than toys. These dolls tended to have, as the example shown here, mask faces of moulded stockinet and painted features. (See also page 21.)

NORAH WELLINGS DOLLS

DATE: **1926–60** NATIONALITY: **English**
MAKER: **Norah Wellings** HEIGHT: **37cm (14½in)**

These two dolls were made by Norah Wellings, who began her career with Chad Valley, before leaving in the mid-1920s to start her own factory with her brother Leonard. An early commission was to make mascot sailor dolls for sale on the Cunard liners, and because these dolls were marked with a small label reading *Made in England by Norah Wellings* her fame soon spread.

Norah Wellings designed dozens of different dolls of different nationalities and sizes. These two examples, which have felt faces and velvet uniforms, represent members of the Women's Royal Air Force (WRAF) and the Women's Royal Naval Service (WRNS), and during World War II Wellings was appointed doll-maker to the British Commonwealth of Nations. As a result, she made many dolls representing members of the many armed services.

WAX DOLLS
. . . .

ENGLISH DOLL

DATE: 18th century NATIONALITY: probably English MAKER: Not known
HEIGHT: 61cm (24in)

This beautiful doll has a wax head, bust and hands, while the rest of the body is of cloth stuffed with straw. The brown eyes are fixed, and the arched eyebrows are indicated by individual indentations in the wax, giving a sophisticated air. (This doll is, in fact, altogether more sophisticated than most other 18th-century dolls.) The thick brown hair is topped by a cap of white muslin, which is decorated with pink ribbons.

The doll wears a fashionable robe of pale turquoise silk, trimmed with ribbons of the same silk. The elbow-length sleeves have double cuffs of pinked ribbons, and the V-neck bodice has detachable white muslin ruffles. The dress is worn over a taffeta waist petticoat, quilted over cream wool, and stays of thick white cotton, stiffened with whalebone, a knee-length linen chemise with full-length sleeves, knitted knee-length wool stockings, and red and gold needlepoint shoes with leather soles.

ENGLISH DOLL

DATE: 1820 NATIONALITY: English MAKER: Not known
HEIGHT: 30cm (12in)

This charming little wax doll has fixed glass eyes and curly brown hair. The light summer dress is made of white cotton, and the large straw sun bonnet ties beneath the chin with a large ribbon bow.

The doll is one of the 1,200 dolls in the collection at the Judges' Lodgings, Lancaster, UK. The Museum of Childhood is on the second floor of the 17th-century building, which was originally used to accommodate visiting circuit judges attending the nearby assizes.

THE PRINCE OF WALES AND PRINCESS ROYAL

DATE: *c*.1843 NATIONALITY: German MAKER: Not known
HEIGHT: left-hand doll 15cm (6in); right-hand doll 16cm (6½in)

There was tremendous interest in the royal family in the 19th century, and these two little dolls, which represent Queen Victoria's two eldest children, were probably sold as souvenirs. They have solid wax heads and limbs. Although they are charming little dolls, no attempt has been made at verisimilitude, and, undressed, the dolls could be anybody.

Albert Edward, the Prince of Wales, later Edward VII, wears a white organza dress, as was customary for baby boys of the period, with a hat of lace and gold, decorated with princely feathers. Victoria, the Princess Royal, the queen's eldest child, who eventually married Frederick III of Germany, wears a lace dress over blue satin and a plaited straw bonnet. Both dolls wear lace pantalettes.

QUEEN VICTORIA

DATE: *c*.1851 NATIONALITY: English MAKER: Not known
HEIGHT: 38cm (15in)

This lovely poured wax model of Queen Victoria as a young woman, wearing coronation robes, was purchased at the Great Exhibition, which was held in London in 1851. It has always been kept under a glass dome, which explains its excellent condition. Although the head, upper torso and arms are of wax, the legs are made of cloth, and the feet, which may be wood, are solid and are covered in bootees, over which are fitted kid shoes.

Beneath the well-fitted and exquisitely trimmed and detailed silk dress, the doll wears a petticoat and pantalettes of pleated lawn. The hair is real, inserted in the wax of the head and braided in the fashion of the time. The eyes are painted blue.

This model resembles another doll representing Queen Victoria, which is in the Museum of London and which is known to be by Madame Augusta Montanari (1818–64). This famous doll-maker was renowned for the excellence of the costumes she provided for her dolls, and this elaborate gown, with its lace and bead trimming, is certainly the work of an experienced and gifted dress-maker.

A M Y

DATE: *c*.1860   NATIONALITY: **English**   MAKER: **Montanari**
HEIGHT: **79cm (31in)**

This doll, known as Amy, is dressed in the authentic mourning dress of a three-year-old child of the 19th century, a period of high mortality rates when children spent much of their young lives dressed in black. Describing this doll, Vivien Greene quoted from *A Manual of Domestic Economy, suited to families spending from £100 to £1000 a year:* "It may . . . be stated as certainly three hundred to one against a death occurring [in childhood] in any young woman of fair average health, who is well formed and who will have the advantage of good nursing and a mind free from care. In those who are not so favourably situated, the mortality is increased to one per cent."

At first Vivien Greene dressed the doll in a Victorian tucked and embroidered white cambric dress to make it look more cheerful, but it later became clear that the original black dress, with the folded crêpe at the sleeves and neckline, was both historically correct and appropriate for the doll.

The fragile arms and legs are hollow-poured wax, and the limbs are attached to the cloth body by metal eyelets. Beneath the dress are a linen chemise, cambric drawers and a petticoat trimmed with heavy, handmade lace. The feet are beautifully moulded with tiny toenails. The pale face, softly coloured mouth and deep eyes with dark lashes convey a sad expression, as befits a mourning doll.

M O N T A N A R I   D O L L

DATE: **1880**   NATIONALITY: **English**   MAKER: **Montanari**
HEIGHT: **71cm (28in)**

This is a fine example of the work of the Montanari family, which was active in London from *c*.1851. The wax lower limbs are attached to the soft body with eyelets. The eyes are fixed, and the hair is inserted. The presence of teeth in a doll of this kind is unusual. The little creases of fat on the neck and around the wrists give a delightful impression of childhood, and the face has such character that it seems likely that it was modelled on a real child. The dress is original to the doll, and is complete to the lace-trimmed drawers, flannel petticoat and all the other Victorian underwear.

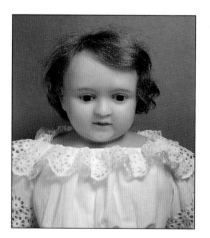

PIEROTTI DOLL

DATE: *c.*1865 NATIONALITY: **English** MAKER: **Pierotti**
HEIGHT: **30cm (12in)**

This doll is attributed to Pierotti, and it bears some resemblance to the doll illustrated below. The colour of the face has faded over the years, but the wax legs and feet, which have always been covered up, are a perfect pink. The doll has inset eyelashes and eyebrows, blue eyes and blond hair. On its body is a stamp reading: "Hamley's Regent Street Doll Emporium". It is fully clothed, down to a flannel petticoat, and has an elaborate bonnet, trimmed with ruching and lace, and a prettily tucked dress.

Pierotti dolls were only rarely marked – the family name is occasionally found incised on the back of the neck – because, as in this case, most London dealers who handled the dolls used their own marks instead.

PIEROTTI DOLL

DATE: *c.*1885 NATIONALITY: **English** MAKER: **Pierotti**
HEIGHT: **51cm (20in)**

The head of this late 19th-century poured wax baby doll is slightly turned to one side, and the delicate features are typical of the work of the Pierotti family, which worked in London from about 1789, making composition and papier mâché dolls as well as finely modelled wax ones. The doll is a fine example of its kind, with inset eyebrows, eyelashes and hair. The bent-limbed body is made of stuffed cloth, but the lower limbs are made of wax. The doll is wearing a tucked and trimmed pelisse and ruched bonnet, both of which are original. When dolls were large enough, they wore real baby clothes.

The baby doll developed slowly through the 19th century, but the style was not mass-produced until Edwardian times. Before then dolls represented miniature adults – and children were regarded in the same way.

CRYING DOLL

DATE: *c.*1870 NATIONALITY: **English**
MAKER: **John Edwards** HEIGHT: **49.5cm (19½in)**

John Edwards (1831–1907) worked in London from about 1868, making a vast range of dolls, from those of high quality to small dolls, made quickly to be sold cheaply. He made dolls for Queen Victoria and exhibited at the London Exhibition of 1871.

The doll illustrated is a rare crying baby doll, with a slightly pink face and an open mouth, showing its tongue. The eyes, with lashes, are closed, and the doll has real blond hair and a cloth body with poured wax lower limbs. It is wearing a long, lace-panelled, pin-tucked christening robe and a cut silk cream bonnet, trimmed with lace.

The realism of the face suggests that Edwards modelled the doll from life, and he may have taken inspiration from his own three daughters. A well-known portrait of his youngest daughter, Maud, which is in the Museum of London, is notable for its realism.

MARSHALL & SNELGROVE DOLL

DATE: *c.*1875 NATIONALITY: **German**
MAKER: **Cuno & Otto Dressel** MARKS: *Holzmasse*
HEIGHT: **61cm (24in)**

This pretty doll was known by its previous owner as the "Marshall & Snelgrove Doll" because it arrived in its original box with the name of the London store on it and the words "child model wax doll". The doll also has its original clothes – a lawn dress with tucks and a lace top, a chemise, three petticoats and split-crutch drawers. The head and shoulders are poured wax, and the arms and legs are of composition. The soft body is stuffed with hair. The mohair curls were inserted into the head, and the doll has fixed blue glass eyes and an open mouth with teeth.

Cuno & Otto Dressel of Sonneberg is one of the earliest doll-making companies for which records exist. The company's best known mark, *Holzmasse* which is on the doll's upper leg, was registered in 1875.

PRINCESS LOUISE

DATE: **1870s** NATIONALITY: **English**
MAKER: **possibly Meech** HEIGHT: **56cm (22in)**

In 1963 Vivien Greene bought a trunkful of clothes, letters, toys, books and other items from the daughter of the head nurse of Marlborough House, once the home of Alexandra, Princess of Wales. Among the fascinating ephemera it contained was this wax portrait doll of Princess Louise, the granddaughter of Queen Victoria, as a child.

The doll is pale, with wax head and limbs and a calico body. Beneath the white dress with its tucked bodice, is a cotton shift, lace-edged drawers, a cream flannel petticoat and a cambric half-petticoat with tucks and lace edging. On the doll's feet are silk shoes and socks, and on the head is a cream silk bonnet. The maker is not known, but is likely to be one of the leading London wax doll-makers of the time. The slightly sulky expression is reminiscent of other dolls made by Meech (see below).

MEECH DOLLS

DATE: *c.*1880 NATIONALITY: **English** MAKER: **Meech**
HEIGHT: **66cm (26in)**

These two dolls were made by the Meech family. Herbert John Meech was doll-maker to the royal family between 1865 and 1891, and the family made composition dolls as well as ones in wax. The family's trademark is stamped on the thigh of the doll wearing the red velvet beret, which matches the cherry red ribbon trimming on the dress. Both dolls have soft brown human hair set in the wax crown, and they share the rather glum expression that characterizes Meech dolls. It is thought that these dolls may have been modelled on one of Herbert Meech's own daughters.

Meech began his career with Madame Tussaud's waxworks when he was about 16 years old. By the time he was 19 in 1852 he had started his own factory in Kennington, southeast London. Three of his children worked for him, and one of them, Ernest, carried on the family business into the 1920s.

CHARLES MARSH DOLL

DATE: *c.*1880 NATIONALITY: **English** MAKER: **Charles Marsh**
HEIGHT: **48cm (19in)**

This Charles Marsh doll is dressed as a bride. The head and hands are of wax, but the generously proportioned body is made of cloth. The hair and eyebrows are inserted in the poured wax head in the traditional way. The fixed glass eyes are blue. The doll bears the maker's stamp on its body and a royal warrant.

Brides were a popular subject for wax doll-makers, probably because they presented an opportunity for pretty dresses and frills and furbelows. It is thought that the clothing on earlier Marsh dolls was made by members of Marsh's family, but little is known about them. Marsh himself produced poured wax and papier mâché dolls between 1878 and about 1894, and the name C. Gooch, who appears to have been Marsh's main distributor, sometimes appears on the maker's stamp. Mary Hillier says that Marsh dolls seem to have a definite neck and a rather erect head, and that particular attention was paid to the ears and hands, which have separate fingers.

LILLIE LANGTRY

DATE: *c.*1900 NATIONALITY: **English** MAKER: **Not known**
HEIGHT: **46cm (18in)**

The maker of this delightful poured wax portrait of Lillie Langtry (1853–1929), the famous Edwardian actress and mistress of Edward VII, is not known. It was given to the owner of the Lilliput Museum by someone who had worked for the actress and who had been given the doll as a memento.

The doll certainly does justice to the beauty of the "Jersey Lily", with her bright blue eyes and flawless complexion. It is, however, probably a somewhat idealized portrait, and it bears little resemblance to the painting of Lillie Langtry by Sir John Millais in the Jersey Museum. The dress worn by the doll appears to be Edwardian, although she was the king's mistress in the 1870s and was an actress in the 1880s. The doll is quite plainly dressed, with a velvet cloak trimmed with fur over a white dress decorated with lace. The hat is decorated with the remains of an ostrich feather.

LORD ROBERTS

DATE: **1901** NATIONALITY: **English** MAKER: **Charles Pierotti**
HEIGHT: **46cm (18in)**

Wax portrait dolls of famous people were as popular with Victorians as were figures of the royal family. Lord Roberts – "Bobs" – was commander-in-chief of the British army during the Boer War, and Charles Pierotti made this lifelike model of the national hero. It is a convincing portrait of a military man at the height of his career, covered in medals (made from toy metal coins), orders and gold braid as befits his rank. The doll has a poured wax head, arms and legs, a stuffed cloth body and glass eyes, and the rather sparse real hair, the eyebrows and the luxuriant moustache are inset. Pierotti also made a similar head portrait of Lord Roberts when he was a general and also a model of Edward VII, 53cm (21in) high, in the uniform of field marshal at his coronation in 1901.

DOLL WITH WATERING CAN

DATE: **1970s** NATIONALITY: **English**
MAKER: **Margaret Glover** HEIGHT: **46cm (18in)**

Margaret Glover is a well-known doll artist who works in London, and she based this doll on a picture by the impressionist painter Renoir. Both painting and doll are now in the USA. The doll is made in the traditional poured wax manner, with inserted hair and eyelashes. The limbs are wax on a fabric body. The dress is of velvet, with antique lace and antique buttons. The leather boots were handmade by Margaret Glover. In fact, Mrs Glover does everything herself, from making the original, casting the wax, inserting the hair and dressing the dolls. She was unable to buy a miniature watering can, so made one out of an empty tube of soldering flux.

WAX-OVER DOLLS

· ·

PRINCESS CAROLINE

DATE: *c.*1790 NATIONALITY: **English** MAKER: **Not known**
HEIGHT: **66cm (26in)**

This wax-over composition doll, which is in
remarkably good condition for its age, is wearing a
dress made by a lady-in-waiting to Princess Caroline
of Brunswick (1768–1821), who was wife of the
Prince Regent, later George IV. For a time, Princess
Caroline was queen of England, although she was
not allowed into Westminster Abbey for the
coronation. Theirs was an unhappy marriage.

The doll's dress is made from a remnant of the
unfortunate woman's wedding dress, a pretty cream,
green and silver brocade, decorated with lace.

The doll is a slit-head – that is, a slit was cut in the
top of the wax-over composition head and hair was
inserted into the slit and allowed to fall down on
either side of the face. The fixed eyes are blue glass,
the arms are wax and the body is cloth.

SLIT-HEAD DOLL

DATE: *c.*1840 NATIONALITY: **English** MAKER: **Not known**
HEIGHT: **66cm (26in)**

Wax is an expensive material, and when dolls began to be mass-
produced in the mid-19th century, ways had to be found to reduce
costs. One of the easiest ways was to dip a cheaper material such as
papier mâché or composition into molten wax, so that the core material
was covered with a thin coating of the expensive wax. This rather
chubby wax-over composition doll has the tell-tale ringlets of the slit-
head doll and also the rather pleased, almost self-satisfied expression
that is often a characteristic of these dolls.

The doll is wearing a lace-trimmed white dress over a complete set of
underwear and a straw bonnet. There is an accompanying trousseau of
seven sets of clothes.

P *UMPKIN-HEAD AND* *B* *ONNET-HEAD* *D* *OLLS*

DATE: **mid-19th century** NATIONALITY: **German** MAKER: **Not known**
HEIGHT: **left-hand doll 46cm (18in); right-hand doll 30cm (12in)**

Both these dolls have wax-over composition heads, but they are made in two contrasting styles.

The left-hand doll is known as a pumpkin-head, a type that is characterized by a broad face and a head that is comparatively flat from back to front. This typical shape results from the rather shallow mould in which the heads were made. The doll has a hair band on the moulded blond hair, and the dark eyes are pupil-less, a style that was popular in the 1860s. The wooden forearms end in carved wooden hands, and the wooden lower legs are finished off with flat-heeled boots with painted buttons. The doll wears a flannel pin-tucked dress over three petticoats and split-crutch drawers.

The right-hand doll is known as a bonnet-head – that is, the hat and hair are moulded with the head. The hat is decorated with three feathers and a snood. The doll has wooden forearms and wooden lower legs, which end in painted flat-heeled boots. The original dress is lawn cotton, and under it are two petticoats. The glass eyes are brown. The doll has what is known as a Motschmann-type body – that is, the upper legs and arms and the centre of the torso are of pieces of fabric, which are attached to the rigid lower limbs, shoulder-plate and pelvis.

S *TRAW-DRESSED* *D* *OLL*

DATE: *c*.**1880** NATIONALITY: **Not known**
MAKER: **Not known** HEIGHT: **23cm (9in)**

This is an unusual doll, with a wax-over composition head, black glass eyes and rather crude composition arms. It is likely that there is a body beneath the elaborate costume, which dates the doll to about 1880. The doll, which is surrounded by straw flowers, wears an elegant outfit of a plaited-straw cape and dress and a straw hat. This doll and several similar dolls may be seen in the Wardown Park Museum, Luton, UK, a town that was the centre of the straw hat-making industry in the 18th and 19th centuries. The origin of these dolls is something of a mystery, as is their nationality, because there are no identifying marks on them. However, they may have been made for a local exhibition of straw work, organized towards the end of the 19th century to encourage the plaiting industry.

BONNET-HEAD DOLL

DATE: **1840–60** NATIONALITY: **probably German** MAKER: **Not known**
HEIGHT: **38cm (15in)**

This is a perfect example of a bonnet-head, wax-over papier mâché doll, on which the hat, complete with its decorative feather, has been moulded with the head.

Bonnet-head dolls can be found with many different styles of hat: some with three feathers, some with a large, single feather, some tricorn-shaped, and some with high crowns. Some bonnet-head dolls were made to represent men and boys.

PRINCESS VICTORIA'S DOLL

DATE: **1845–50** NATIONALITY: **English** MAKER: **Not known**
HEIGHT: **48cm (19in)**

This beautifully dressed wax-over papier mâché doll is said to have belonged to Queen Victoria's eldest daughter, Princess Victoria, the Princess Royal, who was born in 1840. The doll has sleeping eyes, which are worked by a wire hidden in the left wrist. In addition to the well-made dress of shot silk, the doll has been well modelled, and even the finger and toe nails are clearly defined on the wax feet and hands. The real hair has been arranged in pretty ringlets, which fall from a stitched base on the head.

Shoulder-plate Doll

DATE: **mid-19th century** NATIONALITY: **Not known** MAKER: **Not known**
HEIGHT: **Not known**

The wax-over papier mâché shoulder-plate doll has a cloth body that is stuffed with horsehair and arms of maroon leather, which end in four fingers and a thumb. The stuffed feet are rather pigeon-toed. The mohair ringlets are glued to the head. The long pantalettes and cotton dress with blue silk trimming and lace edging and the silk hat are original to the doll. The crazing on the face is often seen on dolls of this kind. Although these dolls, which are sometimes known as "Georgian wax-overs", tend to have somewhat crude forms, with fairly flat faces and rather warped heads (perhaps the result of careless pressing), their blandly smiling faces are not without charm.

German Shoulder-plate Doll

DATE: **1850–55** NATIONALITY: **German**
MAKER: **Not known** HEIGHT: **38cm (15in)**

This handsome wax-over papier mâché doll is wearing a white cotton dress decorated with a tartan trim and pompons. The face is finely modelled and well painted, including the pretty pink cheeks. The brown hair is inserted in the wax, and the brown eyes are glass.

It is easy to see in the illustration where the shoulder-plate ends and joins the fabric of the body, to which the wooden arms are attached.

ENGLISH SLIT-HEAD DOLL

DATE: **mid-19th century** NATIONALITY: **English**
MAKER: **Not known** HEIGHT: **48cm (19in)**

Like the dolls illustrated on page 34, this doll has the characteristic ringlets of a slit-head doll. It is wax-over papier mâché, and the slight crazing on the forehead has been caused by the expansion and contraction of the papier mâché under the wax.

Many dolls of this kind were produced in the first half of the 19th century. Because only the head and shoulder-plate were dipped in wax, while the bodies were made of fabric and the forearms often encased in leather "gloves", they were cheap to make. The more expensive versions would have had wax-over composition limbs. Most dolls of this type have fixed, dark and pupil-less eyes and smiling mouths.

FRENCH WAX-OVER PAPIER MÂCHÉ DOLL

DATE: *c.*1870 NATIONALITY: **French** MAKER: **Not known**
HEIGHT: **73.5cm (29in)**

This large wax-over papier mâché doll is of better quality than the English equivalent illustrated above. The fixed blue eyes have pupils and the mouth is unsmiling, both characteristics suggesting that it is rather later than the English version. In addition, the wax-over papier mâché arms are well shaped, with modelled hands, and the legs, of the same materials, end in neat little red boots. The dress is original to the doll.

BRIDE

DATE: *c.*1880 NATIONALITY: **probably English**
MAKER: **Not known** HEIGHT: **58.5cm (23in)**

This wax-over papier mâché doll has a straw-filled body and rather short composition arms and composition legs. The mohair wig is glued to a carton pate, and the glass eyes are fixed. The bridal gown, underwear, shoes and socks are all original to the doll. The dress is made of oyster paper taffeta and is trimmed with lace. The head-dress and bouquet are adorned with tiny wax flowers.

BARTENSTEIN DOLL

DATE: *c.*1880 NATIONALITY: **German**
MAKER: **Fritz Bartenstein** HEIGHT: **51cm (20in)**

Although Fritz Bartenstein (1839–1913) is perhaps best known for making two-faced dolls, he also made other, less innovative wax dolls, and this exquisite wax-over papier mâché shoulder-head doll is probably one of them. The doll has well-defined fingers, and a pretty, pale face. Two teeth are visible in the open mouth.

PAPIER MÂCHÉ AND COMPOSITION DOLLS

ENGLISH PAPIER MÂCHÉ DOLL

DATE: *c.*1810 NATIONALITY: **English** MAKER: **Not known**
HEIGHT: **27cm (10½in)**

This Regency papier mâché doll has black moulded hair, a leather body and wooden arms. The rather elaborate dress, which is original to the doll, is decorated with a pattern of feathers, and it is trimmed with lace at the neck, sleeves and hem.

Papier mâché dolls with this kind of hair-style are sometimes known as Queen Adelaide dolls, after the wife of William IV, who reigned from 1830 to 1837. Contemporary drawings and paintings show that women did actually wear their hair dressed in this fashion. Between 1810 and 1852 F.G. Volkmar of Ilmenau, Germany, made many of the early types of papier mâché doll heads, with the hair arranged in elaborate swirls and buns moulded into the head and painted black. Head like these are often, for no good reason, called "milliners' models" by collectors, and they are found on a variety of bodies, including calico with kid arms and all-kid with wooden lower limbs. The heads are often found separately and are a desirable addition to any collection.

ENGLISH PAPIER MÂCHÉ DOLL

DATE: *c.*1825 NATIONALITY: **English** MAKER: **Not known**
HEIGHT: **33cm (13in)**

This sumptuously dressed, fine quality papier mâché doll was probably dressed by a professional needlewoman. The bodice is heavily beaded, and the hat, in the fashion of the 1820s, is intricately decorated with ribbons and lace. The doll could, in fact, have been a dress-maker's sample, sent to a wealthy client to demonstrate the maker's skills.

The doll itself has moulded hair and a delicately painted face. The eyes are also painted. The arms are wooden.

GERMAN PAPIER MÂCHÉ DOLL

DATE: *c.*1830 NATIONALITY: **German**
MAKER: **Not known** HEIGHT: **50cm (19½in)**

This fine doll has a papier mâché head and shoulders, attached to a leather body that is stuffed with bran. The real hair has been plaited in an elaborate style, and the glass eyes are fixed. The dress is original to the doll.

Papier mâché, literally "chewed paper", is a paper pulp that is mixed with water to give a lightweight, inexpensive mixture that can be pressed into a mould. Often a filler, such as flour, meal, sand, clay, whiting or chalk, is added to the paper pulp, and the whole is bound together with glue or starch paste. The cost of making a papier mâché doll such as this would have been greater than of making a wooden doll, largely because of the factory overheads, but papier mâché was in itself a cheap substance that lent itself perfectly to the manufacture of dolls, and it continued to be used for limbs even when bisque heads gained ascendancy.

GENERAL VALLÉE DOLL

DATE: **1837** NATIONALITY: **French** MAKER: **Not known**
HEIGHT: **48.5cm (19¼in)**

This elegant doll belonged to the wife of the first French governor of Algeria, General Vallée, in 1837.

The doll's head is papier mâché, but the body is leather. The glass eyes are fixed. The dress is of mousseline (a fine fabric made of rayon or silk) and has leg-of-mutton sleeves, which would have been typical of the light tropical clothing worn by European women in Algeria in the first part of the 19th century.

GREINER DOLL

DATE: *c.*1845 NATIONALITY: **American**

MAKER: **Ludwig Greiner** HEIGHT: **61cm (24in)**

Ludwig Greiner was a German by birth, who emigrated to the USA where he established a factory in Philadelphia to make papier mâché dolls' heads in about 1840. The bodies were often made at home or by local commercial organizations, notably Jacob Lacmann, also of Philadelphia, and so a wide variety of bodies can be found on Greiner heads. Greiner made dolls exclusively for sale in the USA and did not export to Europe. He took out his first patent in March 1858, although heads were made before that date. Some Greiner heads have a paper label bearing the words: *Greiner's Improved Patent Heads/Pat. March 30th '58.*

This rather large doll has moulded hair, painted eyes, leather arms and stuffed legs.

GREINER DOLL

DATE: *c.*1850 NATIONALITY: **American**

MAKER: **Ludwig Greiner** HEIGHT: **29cm (11½in)**

Early papier mâché heads by Ludwig Greiner usually have black hair parted in the centre, like the German bisque dolls of the period, although later heads have different hair-styles. The heads tend to have rather chubby, matronly faces, like this one. Some have glass eyes, but these are painted blue. Greiner tended to apply good varnish to the finished heads, which means that they have lasted better than many dolls made of papier mâchée. Greiner continued to make heads until about 1874, when the company was known as Greiner Brothers. It was taken over by Knell Brothers in 1890.

The doll has a cloth body, leather arms and a patent label, *58,* on the back of the shoulders. The dress, although not original to the doll, is made of old material.

ARMAND MARSEILLE COMPOSITION DOLL

DATE: *c.*1880 NATIONALITY: **German**
MAKER: **Armand Marseille** HEIGHT: **40cm (16in)**

Armand Marseille is better known for the fine bisque heads made in the factories at Köppelsdorf and Neuhaus, but this bent-limbed baby doll is made of composition. In fact, Marseille continued to produce dolls' heads in a kind of non-breakable composition known as Marsit and in pressed composition until 1937.

This doll has an open mouth and dark blue, sleeping eyes, and it is wearing a white tucked christening robe and a fur-trimmed bonnet. It was once offered to Queen Victoria as a gift for one of her children, but she ungraciously refused it.

FAIRY DOLL

DATE: *c.*1911 NATIONALITY: **American** MAKER: **E.I. Horsman & Co.**
HEIGHT: **33cm (13in)**

Edward I. Horsman, a US toy distributor, began to import toys from Europe in the 1870s, and by 1900 his New York company was making toys and dolls as well. The Fairy, which was designed by Helen Trowbridge, was registered by Horsman in 1911. It represents the figure advertised by N.K. Fairbanks Co. for its Little Fairy Soap.

In 1909 Horsman had secured rights to produce the Aetna Company's "Can't Break 'Em" composition dolls' heads, which were described as being "modelled from life by an American sculptress and such original models duly protected by copyright". The ingredients and method of manufacture of the composition were a closely guarded secret.

BUBBLES

DATE: 1925 NATIONALITY: **American** MAKER: **Effanbee**
HEIGHT: **36cm (14in)**

Fleischaker & Baum was founded in New York City by Bernard E. Fleischaker and Hugo Baum, who registered the name Effanbee as their trademark in 1913. The company, which is better known as Effanbee, produced a wide variety of dolls, including a range of "unbreakable" composition dolls. (See also page 71.)

Bubbles was registered in 1925. It is an all-composition doll, wearing the original dress and bonnet, and a pair of knitted bootees. This series of dolls had cry voices, open mouths, in which two teeth are visible, elongated bodies and well-defined dimples.

ROSI

DATE: 1930s NATIONALITY: **German** MAKER: **Not known**
MARKS: **Rosi on back of neck** HEIGHT: **43cm (17in)**

This charming composition doll, wearing its original 1930s clothes and original luxuriant wig, was made in Germany. There are joints at neck, shoulders, wrists, hips and elbows and the name *Rosi* is scratched on the back of the neck.

According to Jürgen and Marianne Cieslik the tradename *Rosi* was used by Kämmer & Reinhardt in 1929. An advertisement for a range of dolls with sleeping eyes included the words: "Unbreakable rosy 'Panta' heads, 'Rosi' heads, breakable like porcelain, 'Roli' celluloid heads.' This doll could certainly have been part of that famous company's range.

SHIRLEY TEMPLE

DATE: **1934–9**   NATIONALITY: **American**
MAKER: **Ideal Novelty & Toy Co.**
MARKS: *13 Shirley Temple*   HEIGHT: **33cm (13in)**

There must have been dozens of different doll
versions of the child star of the 1930s. This version,
by the Ideal Novelty & Toy Co., of Brooklyn, New
York, which is wearing its original dress and wig,
does not resemble her as much as some other dolls,
and the star's characteristic curly hair seems to have
straightened over the years. Ideal registered the
design in the 1930s, and it was one of the
company's most successful dolls. The company was
founded *c.*1906 by Morris Mitchom, and it was
making unbreakable composition dolls by 1909.
Ideal reissued this doll in the 1950s in hard plastic
and vinyl.

POST-WAR DOLLS

DATE: **1950s**   NATIONALITY: **English**   HEIGHT: **30–43cm (12–17in)**

The large doll with the crazed face is a composition bent-
limbed baby with sleeping eyes by the UK company Pedigree.
The doll on the left and the one at centre front are pot-head
dolls with bent limbs; the doll on the left has cloth limbs and
the line of the mould in which the head was cast is visible
running down the side of the head. The doll on the right, with

blond mohair plaits, is made of cloth.
Pedigree Dolls & Toys Ltd, of Canterbury, was founded in
1938 and it was the first company in the UK to mass-produce
high quality composition dolls, which were advertised as
'almost unbreakable'. All the dolls have joints at shoulders
and hips. (See also page 75.)

PARIAN AND GLAZED CHINA DOLLS

PARIAN SHOULDER-PLATE DOLL

DATE: *c.*1850 NATIONALITY: **German**
MAKER: **Not known** HEIGHT: **42cm (16½in)**

The word Parian comes from the name of the Greek island of Paros, where white marble was found. The fine white bisque known as Parian was used for ornaments and statues as well as for dolls from *c.*1850 to *c.*1880. Parian-headed dolls are generally regarded as having been made in Germany, and they are usually blond, the pale yellow showing up well against the white bisque.

This exquisite example has an elaborate moulded hair-style and hair ribbon, a moulded ribbon around the neck and even a moulded bodice on the shoulder-plate. Because Parian bisque is fine enough to pick up small details from the mould, many dolls in this material have dress details incorporated in the moulded design. The doll has leather arms. The ears are pierced to hold earrings, and the blue eyes are painted. The dress is modern.

FLORAL DOLL

DATE: *c.*1850 NATIONALITY: **German** MAKER: **Not known**
HEIGHT: **28cm (11in)**

This pretty Parian doll with moulded flowers, a necklace picked out in lustre and white Parian lower limbs, is wearing a white dress with embroidered swags of roses around the hem. The fair hair is moulded. Although Parian and china dolls are somewhat similar, and indeed, it is believed that the same moulds were often used for both materials, the Parian dolls are usually much more elaborately decorated.

PRINCESS AUGUSTA VICTORIA

DATE: **1870** NATIONALITY: **German** MAKER: **Not known**
HEIGHT: **30cm (12in)**

This rare and beautiful unglazed Parian shoulder-head doll is known as Princess Augusta Victoria. The moulded, elaborate hair is decorated with a sort of bead tiara, and the ears are pierced. Also moulded with the shoulder-head are the ruffled collar and necklace with its pendant cross. The face painting on Parian dolls is usually of the same high quality as on this example. The eyes of this doll are, as is customary, painted blue, but these dolls are occasionally seen with brown eyes and a few have glass eyes.

COUNTESS DAGMAR

DATE: **1870** NATIONALITY: **German** MAKER: **Not known**
HEIGHT: **43cm (17in)**

Countess Dagmar has finely modelled and detailed hair with plenty of curls. The blouse, with its high neckline and row of buttons, also reveals the care with which the mould was prepared. The blue painted eyes have red eye dots and a red upper line. The fabric body is stuffed, and the doll has bisque arms and lower legs with black painted boots, red laces and, unusually, blue painted garters. The dress does not do justice to such a lovely doll. It was probably made by a child with whatever material was available.

PINK LUSTRE CHINA HEAD

DATE: *c.*1840   NATIONALITY: **German**   MAKER: **Not known**   HEIGHT: 15cm (6in)

This early pink lustre china head has pink cheeks and well-detailed dark brown ringlets. The pink glaze was applied after the colouring to give a rosy glow to the head, a technique that continued to be used until the 1900s.

The sewing holes are thought by some collectors to be an indication of the age of a doll, and it has been suggested that those with three holes are earlier than those with two. This is not a reliable yardstick, however, and because these heads are unmarked, dating them is largely a matter of guesswork.

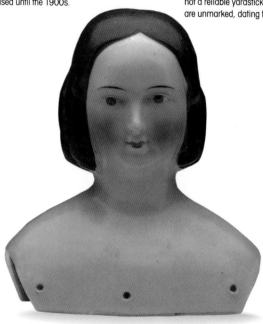

CHINA HEADS

DATE: **left-hand head *c.*1890; right-hand head *c.*1880**
NATIONALITY: **German**   MAKER: **Not known**
HEIGHT: **10cm (4in)**

The black hair of both these china dolls' heads is painted. The shoulder-plate on the left has two holes for attaching the shoulder-plate to a soft body, while the right-hand doll has three holes. The left-hand doll has a "low-brow" moulded hair-style and blue painted eyes with a red eyelid line. The right-hand doll has a more unusual hair-style, taken back behind the ears.

CHINA HEADS

DATE: left-hand head 1890–1900; right-hand head c.1880 NATIONALITY: German MAKER: Not known
HEIGHT: left-hand head 15cm (6in); right-hand head 12cm (4¾in)

Low-brow glazed china heads became more and more popular as the 19th century wore on, and these two examples have blond painted hair. The shades of blondness varied from honey colour to light brown, and the faces became more child-like towards the end of the century, having plump cheeks and rather short necks.

The features on the left-hand head have been well painted, with a red line added above the eyes. The ears on the right-hand doll are partly showing, and this type of head, with its shorter hair, was often used on dolls dressed as boys or men.

BONNET-HEAD

DATE: Late 19th century NATIONALITY: German MAKER: Not known
MARKS: 27 HEIGHT: 6cm (2½in)

This moulded china bonnet-head doll has blue painted eyes, and the china itself has a bluish tinge. The brim of the sun bonnet-type hat is orange, there is a blue bow under the chin, and the hat has a pink bow on top.

Bonnet dolls, wearing different styles of hat, were made from about 1860 to 1930, and this particular style was made famous by the artist and book illustrator Kate Greenaway (1846–1901).

DANISH DOLL

DATE: **1840s** NATIONALITY: **Danish**
MAKER: **Royal Copenhagen** HEIGHT: **34cm (13½in)**

This lovely china-head doll by Royal Copenhagen dates from the 1840s. These heads were produced only from c.1843 until 1880, and only about 23,000 heads were made. These were marked with three lines inside the breastplate. The brownish-black hair is intertwined in a bun at the centre back of the head, and at the back of the exposed part of the ear is a lock of hair ending in brush marks. The eyes are painted blue, and the eyebrows are brown. The feet are exceptionally well modelled. The body is of cloth.

MEISSEN DOLL

DATE: **1840** NATIONALITY: **German** MAKER: **KPM**
MARKS: *KPM* **under an orb surmounted by a cross**
HEIGHT: **44cm (17½in)**

Königliche Porzellanmanufaktur at Meissen was the first porcelain manufactory to be established (1710) after the invention of porcelain by Friedrich Wilhelm Böttger (1682–1719). In addition to its usual range of domestic wares, the Meissen factory made dolls' heads of exceptionally fine quality in the first half of the 19th century. This glazed china shoulder-head has dark moulded hair, blue painted eyes and a closed mouth. The colouring of the face of this beautiful doll is particularly subtle. Note how the corners of the eyes are indicated by a red dot, as are the insides of the nostrils. The forearms are of leather, and this doll represents a grown woman rather than a child.

EMPRESS EUGÉNIE

DATE: *c.*1860 NATIONALITY: **German**
MAKER: **Not known** HEIGHT: **41cm (16¼in)**

This late 19th-century glazed china doll represents the Empress Eugénie of France (1826–1920), a noted beauty of her day, with a flair for dressing in glamorous clothes. This doll is wearing a silk gown, trimmed with lace, and with a blue embroidered train. There is a complete set of undergarments, including a trimmed and a plain calico petticoat, a petticoat of nun's veiling, pantalettes and a front-buttoning chemisette.

The doll has a white glazed china face with tinted rosy cheeks and painted black hair and eyebrows, and painted black boots. The porcelain lower arms and legs are attached to pink cloth upper limbs, which, in turn, are attached to a pink cloth body. The ears are pierced to hold earrings.

FROZEN CHARLOTTES

DATE: *c.*1890–1920s NATIONALITY: **German**
MAKER: **Not known** HEIGHT: **1.5–46cm (½–18in)**

The sophisticated casting methods that had developed by the end of the 19th century made it possible to produce china dolls with limbs. These were known as frozen Charlottes, pillar dolls, bathing babies and solid chinas. Most have clenched fists and bent elbows, and they have no joints. They are usually girls, ranging in size from the very small to the comparatively large, they were of glazed china, either white or tinted pink, and they had moulded hair-styles and facial features. They are very occasionally found with moulded clothes, and sometimes moulded boots. The smallest ones were sometimes used in cakes and Christmas puddings as surprise trinkets.

BISQUE DOLLS

ROHMER FASHION DOLL

DATE: **1857–70** NATIONALITY: **French** MAKER: **Rohmer**
MARKS: *Mme Rohmer Breveté SGDG Paris*
HEIGHT: **51cm (20in)**

Dolls made by Rohmer are highly sought after by collectors. Between *c.*1858 and 1880 Mme Marie Antoinette Leontine Rohmer made and sold dolls in Paris. She obtained patents for jointed dolls and for dolls that had cords running from the head and for attaching ribbons to eyelets in the abdomen to allow dolls' knees to bend. The maker's mark is stamped on the body in green. This doll has a swivel head with a real hair wig, the forearms are glazed porcelain and the body is leather. The upper arms and legs are ball and socket jointed wood covered with leather. Although this doll is of the type generally described as a fashion doll, and the face is certainly typical of a fashion doll, the dress is that of a child.

GAULTIER FASHION DOLL

DATE: *c.*1870 NATIONALITY: **French** MAKER: **Gaultier**
MARKS: *F.G.4* HEIGHT: **44cm (17½in)**

The initials *F.G.* indicate that this doll is probably the work of Fernand Gaultier. It has a bisque swivel head and shoulder-plate and a leather, gusseted body. The wig is real hair.

Gaultier worked in Paris between 1860 and about 1916, and his company exhibited dolls' heads at the Paris Exhibition in 1878, when a silver medal was won. The company won many more awards, and it supplied heads to other doll-makers as well as making whole dolls themselves. The initials *F.G.* sometimes appear on dolls by Gesland, to whom Gaultier supplied heads and who was active at the same period.

ROCHARD FASHION DOLL

DATE: **1867–77** NATIONALITY: **French** MAKER: **Rochard**
MARKS: *Ed Rochard* HEIGHT: **64cm (26in)**

This rare bisque-headed doll with a kid body, wooden arms and pale complexion bears the signature of E. Rochard. There is, however, no record of any doll-maker of that name, and the doll could be by any one of several well-known French makers of that period. Nevertheless, the necklace worn by the doll is of great interest, and it enables the doll to be dated to between 1867 and 1877. The necklace consists of 22 convex glass insets or Stanhopes, each of which contains a tiny photograph. Stanhopes were named after their inventor, Charles, 3rd Earl of Stanhope. They are actually lenses, into which photographs have been embedded, and these are inserted into holes in the shoulder-plate, where they are glued in place.

The photographs can be viewed by holding the doll up to the light at a certain angle, when they catch the light coming from a cut-away section at the back of the shoulder-plate. When the eye is placed to the convex surface, the lens magnifies the photograph beneath it. The photographs are of places of tourist interest in Paris, Geneva and Venice, with the addition of six religious scenes in the cross. Edmond Rochard took out a 15-year patent for Stanhopes in 1867, intending them to be inserted into dolls, toys and religious objects.

The doll also has slightly parted lips to allow for the viewing of a kaleidoscope inside the doll's head, which was to be hidden by the hair.

STEINER BÉBÉ

DATE: **1880s** NATIONALITY: **French** MAKER: **Steiner**
HEIGHT: **46cm (18in)**

Jules Nicholas Steiner founded the company known as Société Steiner in Paris in 1855, and it specialized in mechanical bébés, which walked and talked. Steiner claimed, in fact, to have invented the bébé (a doll representing a child aged about eight years), and although this cannot be substantiated, the firm was certainly among the first to produce this type of doll and in considerable number. Although Steiner is perhaps best remembered for its walking dolls, patented in 1890, it also made some beautiful open-closed mouth bébés, such as this one. The doll has fixed violet eyes, a jointed composition body and pierced ears. It is wearing its original wig and clothes.

BRU FASHION DOLL

DATE: *c.*1880 NATIONALITY: **French** MAKER: **Bru**
MARKS: **Circle and dot** HEIGHT: **61cm (24in)**

Dolls made by Bru Jne & Cie are among the finest of all French dolls – they are beautiful to look at and beautifully made. The bodies are often of gusseted leather, with bisque or sometimes carved wooden lower limbs. The swivel heads are well modelled, with slightly parted lips and delicate colour. Some of the early Bru dolls are marked only with a circle and a dot, like this one, which has a leather body, porcelain hands and leather feet. The mouth is open-closed – that is, the lips are slightly parted – and the blue eyes are fixed. The doll is wearing its original wig, a navy blue velvet dress trimmed with cream lace and a straw hat trimmed with roses.

BRU BÉBÉ

DATE: *c.*1880 NATIONALITY: **French** MAKER: **Bru**
MARKS: *Bru Jne* 9 HEIGHT: **51cm (20in)**

This Bru bébé is dressed in elaborate child's clothing. It has brown eyes and an open-closed mouth and its original blond mohair wig. The mark is incised on the head and on the shoulder-plate. The doll has a swivel head, a kid body, bisque forearms and wooden lower legs. The delicate painting of the facial features is characteristic of the maker.

SCHMITT BÉBÉ

DATE: **late 1870s** NATIONALITY: **French** MAKER: **Schmitt et Fils**
MARKS: *SCH3* HEIGHT: **48cm (19in)**

This closed-mouth bébé has a bisque head, blue glass eyes, lambswool hair and a ball-jointed body. Schmitt et Fils of Paris made dolls between about 1863 and 1891. The company advertised its indestructible jointed bébé, called Bébé Schmitt, from 1879 to 1890, about the same time that Jumeau and other French companies were making their own child dolls. The large eyes, rosebud mouth and chubby chin are typical of Schmitt dolls, as are the dolls' flat bottoms, which enable them to sit easily. The mark is in the hollow of the doll's head. Schmitt also sometimes used the symbol of crossed keys above the initials *SCH*, all within a shield.

HURET MALE DOLL

DATE: **late 19th century** NATIONALITY: **French**
MAKER: **Maison Huret** MARKS: *Huret, rue de la Boetie*
HEIGHT: **left-hand doll 52cm (20½in); right-hand doll 47cm (18½in)**

This is an unusual male doll, complete with beard and moustache; the wig is not original. The doll is marked on the back of the body, which is made of jointed wood, and the hands are metal. Maison Huret of Paris made a variety of dolls from about 1850 to at least the 1920s. The doll and its companion are shown in a scene entitled "Chez Alfred de Musset", but the poet was not married, so the bisque fashion doll on the right may simply be representing a visitor.

The fashion doll has a gusseted kid body and blue eyes and is dressed in a velvet coat over a yellow satin dress. The doll has a swivel head on a bisque shoulder-plate, a blond wig fashioned in a plait around the head, pierced ears, from which hang blue earrings, and kid hands, on which the fingers are indicated. Although the doll is unmarked, it may also be by Huret.

RABERY & DELPHIEU FASHION DOLL

DATE: *c.*1880 NATIONALITY: **French**
MAKER: **Rabery & Delphieu** HEIGHT: **36cm (14in)**

The bisque head of this fashion doll has a closed mouth, and the composition body is jointed. The doll is wearing an outfit of a style that was fashionable in the late 19th century.

Rabery & Delphieu made dolls in Paris from 1856 until 1899, when it joined the SFBJ. At first it made fashion dolls, with bisque heads and either cloth or kid bodies, and later began to make bébés with jointed bodies. The company also made some innovative dolls, including ones that said "Mama" and "Papa" when a string was pulled, for which it used a type of composition.

DENAMUR BÉBÉ

DATE: *c.*1910 NATIONALITY: **French** MAKER: **probably E. Denamur** MARKS: *E 11 D* HEIGHT: **51cm (20in)**

The bisque head of this bébé has an open mouth in which teeth are visible. The body is of jointed composition.

The doll can only be attributed to E. Denamur (or Denamour), who made dolls in Paris from about 1867, since the initials *ED* were also used by doll-makers Emile Douillet, E. Dumont and E. Daspres. Dolls bearing this mark are characterized by the eyebrows, which almost meet in the centre.

JUMEAU FASHION DOLL

DATE: **Late 19th century**   NATIONALITY: **French**
MAKER: **probably Jumeau**   HEIGHT: **30cm (12in)**

Although it is unmarked, this doll is of the high quality associated with Jumeau. The firm of Belton & Jumeau was established in 1843, and after Belton's death, Pierre François Jumeau opened a factory of his own in Montreuil in 1873. On Pierre's retirement, his son Emile took over the company in 1877, and under his management the firm was awarded five gold medals and a silver medal at international exhibitions.

The head, hands and arms are bisque, the body is kid and the blue eyes are glass. The eyebrows are clearly defined, the neat mouth is closed and the face is beautifully painted. The doll is wearing a cream silk bridal dress and a bridal wreath in its blond hair, and the dress is of the fine quality that is found on other Jumeau "Parisiennes" or fashion dolls.

JUMEAU BÉBÉ

DATE: **c.1880**   NATIONALITY: **French**   MAKER: **Jumeau**
HEIGHT: **61cm (24in)**

This very pretty Jumeau bébé has fixed paperweight eyes and an open-closed mouth. Although unmarked, it is typical of the many fine bébés that were produced by Jumeau towards the end of the 19th century. Although Emile Jumeau once claimed that every doll that left the factory bore the Jumeau name or mark, production increased dramatically towards the end of the century, and many dolls were not marked. It has been said that in 1881 alone Jumeau sold 85,000 dolls. In addition, Jumeau imported Simon & Halbig heads from Germany, and although some authorities suggest that the German company reserved the mould numbers in the 200s for Jumeau, this alone cannot be a guarantee of authenticity.

SFBJ CHARACTER DOLL

DATE: *c.*1910 NATIONALITY: **French** MAKER: **SFBJ**
MARKS: *SFBJ 250 Paris 1 SO* HEIGHT: **57cm (22½in)**

The Société Française de Fabrication de Bébés et Jouets (SFBJ) was founded in 1899 by French doll manufacturers who found themselves unable to compete with the fine dolls that were being mass-produced more economically in Germany. The original members of the SFBJ were Bru, Fleischmann & Bloedel, Gaultier (then known as a porcelain manufacturer), Genty, Girard, Gobert, Jumeau, Pintel & Godchaux, Rabery & Delphieu and Remignard. Later, A. Bouchet and P.H. Schmitz joined, as did, in 1911, Daniel & Cie. Most SFBJ dolls were bébés with bisque heads (some of which were imported from Simon & Halbig) on jointed composition bodies, but some character dolls were produced.

This bisque head doll has an open mouth showing the upper teeth, a dimple in the chin, weighted blue glass, flirty eyes, pierced ears and an auburn wig of real hair. The body is of composition with jointed wood limbs. The smart navy blue sailor suit is not original to the doll, but it was made from old fabrics. The doll is also wearing long leather boots.

SFBJ FASHION DOLL

DATE: *c.*1925 NATIONALITY: **French** MAKER: **SFBJ**
HEIGHT: **51cm (20in)**

This doll is dressed in a costume that was the height of fashion in the 1920s, and although it is unmarked, it was probably one of the millions of dolls produced by the SFBJ's eight factories at this period. The doll has a bisque head on a swivel neck and a composition body with jointed wooden limbs, including joints at the wrists. Note the careful modelling of the fingers. Four teeth are visible in the open mouth.

ALBERT MARQUE DOLL

DATE: *c.*1913 NATIONALITY: **French** MAKER: **Albert Marque**
HEIGHT: **55cm (21½in)**

The model for this rare and lovely doll was made by the French sculptor Albert Marque (1872–1939). Very few of his dolls are known. There are five in the Carnegie Museum, Pittsburgh, USA, and one in the Margaret Woodbury Strong Museum, New York. Marque made many sculptures of children's heads and some dolls, which were sold in Paris. The dolls, which are all the same size, were made from the same mould, and they have the same composition body with bisque forearms. They have closed mouths, blue or brown paperweight eyes and an incised signature on the back of the neck. This doll is wearing its original wig and dress, with a yellow jacket faced with the same fabric as the dress.

In their book *How to Collect French Bébé Dolls* Mildred and Vernon Seeley, the owners of the doll shown here, include a photograph of a terracotta bust of a young girl by Marque in the Musée des Arts Décoratifs, Paris, signed and dated 1913. They feel that their Marque doll was made at the same time as the bust because it is an exact reproduction of it.

LANTERNIER CHARACTER DOLL

DATE: **1915** NATIONALITY: **French**
MAKER: **A. Lanternier & Cie**
MARKS: *Favorite no. 2/0/ A.L. & Cie*
HEIGHT: **41cm (16¼in)**

The bisque heads of Lanternier, which were made at the company's factory at Limoges between 1891 and about 1925, have been found with the incised name *Favorite*, *Lorraine* or *La Georgienne*. This doll was designed by the sculptor J.E. (or T.E.) Maskon (or Masson), who made wax and clay models for art dolls and whose signature appears on the back of the doll's neck. His signature has also been found on dolls' heads made by Couty, Magne & Cie. (also known as Coiffe), another Limoges manufacturer. Some Lanternier heads bear the signature of Ed. Tasson, whose identity is uncertain.

This doll, which is wearing neither its original wig nor its original dress, has fixed eyes, heavily painted eyebrows, a dark red open mouth, revealing upper teeth, and pierced ears. The jointed body and limbs are of composition.

HEUBACH CHARACTER DOLL

DATE: *c*.1900 NATIONALITY: **German** MAKER: **Gebrüder Heubach**
HEIGHT: **18cm (7in)**

The porcelain factory at Lichte was bought by the Heubach family in 1840, and soon after this date porcelain figurines were made. The beautiful bisque heads with intaglio eyes are not recorded as having been produced before the 1910s, when the square *HEUBACH* trademark was registered. The company is famous for character dolls, piano babies (ornaments in the shape of babies) and other ornamental pieces. This small character doll has a closed mouth, painted intaglio eyes, a composition body and bent limbs. The knitted romper suit is new, but the shift is original. Dolls made by Gebrüder Heubach are also sometimes marked with the company's well-known rising sun mark.

Gebrüder Heubach dolls should not be confused with those produced by Ernst Heubach of Köppelsdorf, who founded a porcelain factory in 1887 to manufacture bisque dolls' heads and frozen Charlottes and who made a range of character dolls after about 1910; the company merged with Armand Marseille in 1919 but the two businesses separated in 1932. A third German doll-maker of this name was Friedrich A. Heubach of Sonneberg, whose company was taken over in 1900 by Otto Reupke; the company was advertising dolls with movable eyelids and dressed and undressed dolls in the 1920s.

HANDWERCK CHARACTER DOLL

DATE: **1902** NATIONALITY: **German** MAKER: **Max Handwerck**
HEIGHT: **68.5cm (27in)**

This Max Handwerck doll has brown eyes, an open mouth, showing top teeth, and a composition body and composition arms and legs. The dress, lace bonnet and yellow shoes with bows are original to the doll. Max Handwerck founded the company that bears his name at Waltershausen in 1899. The company made porcelain and bisque dolls, doll parts and clothes, and it used dolls' heads supplied by the factory of F. & W. Goebel at Oeslau, which made the bisque heads to Max Handwerck's own moulds.

Also at Waltershausen was the doll-making factory of Heinrich Handwerck, which was founded in 1886 to produce a range of ball-jointed dolls. These dolls often had heads made by Simon & Halbig.

RECKNAGEL CHARACTER DOLL

DATE: **1907** NATIONALITY: **German** MAKER: **Theodor Recknagel**
MARKS: *DEP R/Recknagel 1907* HEIGHT: **15cm (6in)**

Theodor Recknagel (1860–1930) produced bisque heads between c.1893 and c.1930 at a factory at Alexandrienthal. This small doll has an open mouth with teeth, fixed eyes, a straight-limbed, composition body jointed at hips and shoulders and a swivel neck. The hair is original to the doll, which is wearing a felt jacket, a lace shirt and velvet trousers. The shoes are painted. After World War I the factory also made composition heads.

GEBRUDER HEUBACH CHARACTER DOLLS

DATE: **1912–14** NATIONALITY: **German**
MAKER: **Gebruder Heubach**
HEIGHT: **centre doll 36cm (14in)**

In the late 19th and early 20th centuries more realistic looking dolls began to be made, and artists were commissioned by different doll-making companies to model the heads. This group shows some of the dolls produced by Gebrüder Heubach just before World War I.

The doll on the left has an open-closed mouth showing its tongue. The rather contorted expression suggests that of a crying child. The hair is moulded, and the wood and composition body is jointed. The doll in the centre has bent limbs, and open-closed mouth showing two lower teeth, weighted blue glass eyes and a real hair wig. The doll on the right is a smiling open-closed mouth doll, showing a moulded tongue. The hair is moulded, and the wood and composition body is jointed. The intaglio eyes are looking to the left.

SIMON & HALBIG FASHION DOLL

DATE: *c.*1880 NATIONALITY: **German** MAKER: **Simon & Halbig**
MARKS: *S 6 H* HEIGHT: **40cm (16in)**

Simon & Halbig was (after Armand Marseille) the second largest producer of dolls' heads in Germany. The company was founded at Gräfenheim in 1869 by Wilhelm Simon (d.1894) and Carl Halbig (1839–1926) to manufacture porcelain, but because Simon was also a maker of toys, the company began to make bisque heads both for its own dolls and for other doll-making companies.

This charming doll has blue glass eyes and wears a blond wig. The ears are pierced. The doll's body is of fabric, and the arms are bisque. Contemporary with the doll but not original to it is the smart two-piece dress, which has a small bustle, a matching hat and gold leather boots with heels.

SIMON & HALBIG CHILD DOLL

DATE: **1899** NATIONALITY: **German**
MAKER: **Simon & Halbig** HEIGHT: **61cm (24in)**

Simon & Halbig made a wide range of baby, child and lady dolls, and also character dolls and dolls with moulded hair-styles. The designers, modellers and painters employed by the company were among the most skilled in the entire German doll-making industry, and the quality of the bisque was exceptionally high.

This rather lovely doll, which is holding a small teddy bear, was sold to the Lilliput Museum by the original owner, who had been given the doll when she was three years old. The doll has a pink leather body, upper and lower limbs of bisque, and a swivel neck on a shoulder-plate. The dark brown eyes are fixed, and the original hair is real. The doll is wearing the white cotton dress with lace inserts in which it was dressed by its first owner, but it seems unlikely that the doll would have been sold wearing such a fine garment.

KÄMMER & REINHARDT CHARACTER DOLL

DATE: *c.*1910 NATIONALITY: **German**
MAKER: **Kämmer & Reinhardt** HEIGHT: 28cm (11in)

The company founded at Waltershausen in 1886 by the designer and modeller Ernst Kämmer and the businessman Franz Reinhardt proved to be one of the most successful in the history of doll-making. The famous character dolls, *Charakterpuppe*, were introduced in 1909, when Reinhardt saw the art dolls of Marion Kaulitz at an exhibition in Munich. He commissioned a Berlin artist to make a new style of baby mould – it was based on a six-week-old infant – and then there followed a long line of named dolls, ranging from babies to older children of both sexes, with a variety of facial expressions.

This character baby has painted, moulded hair and an open mouth, in which the tongue is visible. The body has bent limbs, and there are dimples on the knees and the creases and rolls of fat that would be seen on a real baby.

ELISE

DATE: *c.*1910 NATIONALITY: **German**
MAKER: **Kämmer & Reinhardt** MARKS: *109*
HEIGHT: **46cm (18in)**

This toddler doll, mould number 109 in Kämmer & Reinhardt's series, is known as Elise, and the style was first made in 1909. The doll has painted intaglio eyes, an open-closed mouth and a jointed composition body. The company named the boy version of this mould Walter.

KESTNER FASHION DOLL

DATE: late 19th century NATIONALITY: German
MAKER: Probably Kestner MARKS: *139*
HEIGHT: 34cm (13½in)

This bisque shoulder-plate doll with a closed mouth has a leather body, bisque arms and fixed blue paperweight eyes. The mark is somewhat indistinct, but it seems likely that this doll was made by Kestne specifically for the French market. Johann Daniel Kestner founded a papier mâché factory at Waltershausen in 1816. Production increased steadily, and by the mid-1860s the company was producing a huge range of wax, porcelain, bisque, wood and composition dolls as well as doll parts. In addition to making its own range, Kestner worked with other German and some US companies, supplying bodies and doll parts. The factory closed in 1938.

KESTNER CHARACTER DOLL

DATE: early 20th century NATIONALITY: German
MAKER: Kestner MARKS: *DRGM 4428107*
HEIGHT: 36cm (14in)

This boy character doll has the J.D. Kestner mould number 142. The doll has a jointed, sawdust-filled, leather body and upper arms and legs, and composition lower arms and legs. The unusual jointing method by which leather meets composition is visible in the doll's left arm. The doll's intaglio eyes are painted, and it has painted moulded hair. The clothes are not original to the doll.

F. & W. GOEBEL DOLL

DATE: *c.*1910–15 NATIONALITY: **German** MAKER: **Goebel**
HEIGHT: **46cm (18in)**

Franz Detleff Goebel and his son William established
a porcelain factory at Oeslau in 1867, and by the
1880s the company was producing dolls' heads for
other doll manufacturers, including Max Handwerck
(see page 60). In 1893 William Goebel became sole
proprietor of the company, which, by the end of the
century, was making over 100 shoulder-head,
socket-head and straight neck dolls' heads, some in
up to 21 sizes. When William Goebel died in 1911,
his son Max Louis took over the company, and the
company's range extended into all-bisque dolls,
porcelain dolls and dolls' heads. This cheerful
looking doll has a bisque head with an open mouth
and a bent-limbed composition baby body.

The small doll in front is 18cm (7in) tall. It has a
bisque head with a flange neck, closing eyes, a
closed mouth, a cloth body and composition hands.
It was made by Hermann Steiner of Neustadt, a
company founded in 1920.

PRINCESS ELIZABETH

DATE: **1929** NATIONALITY: **German**
MAKER: **Schoenau & Hoffmeister**
MARKS: **Porzellanfabrik Burggrub**
HEIGHT: **61cm (24in)**

The company of Schoenau & Hoffmeister was founded
in Burggrub in 1901. It manufactured porcelain and
supplied bisque dolls' heads to the Sonneberg factory of
Arthur Schoenau.

This doll is a portrait of the three-year-old Princess
Elizabeth, and it is the largest mould size – 6½ –
produced by the factory. The body is that of a straight-
limbed toddler, and it has its original mohair wig, blue
glass sleeping eyes and an open mouth with teeth.

Dolls by Schoenau & Hoffmeister are sometimes
confused with those by Simon & Halbig because of the
shared initials, but the Burggrub company sign includes
a large star between the *S* and *H*, while Simon & Halbig
used the simple *S&H* or an *S* and *H* separated by a
mould or size number.

M Y D R E A M B A B Y

DATE: *c.*1920 NATIONALITY: **German** MAKER: **Armand Marseille**
MARKS: *AM 341–6K* HEIGHT: **46cm (18in)**

In 1884 Armand Marseille bought a toy factory and the next year he bought a porcelain factory, but it was not until *c.*1890 that his factories at Köppelsdorf and Neuhaus began to produce shoulder-heads. Marseille made bisque heads both for his own dolls and for other doll-making companies. The numbering system adopted does not appear to have been systematically applied, and identification is often further complicated by the variety of marks used by Armand Marseille and by the fact that the initials *AM* were often used with the marks of the companies for which Marseille provided heads. However, the *AM* that appears on practically every head made by the company is unmistakable. The mould number 341 was first used in 1913, and the doll is known as My Dream Baby, a name registered in the USA in 1925. This doll has a bisque head with a flange neck and domed head blue sleeping eyes and a closed mouth. The bent-limbed body is composition. Black and mulatto versions were also made. The doll illustrated is wearing its original clothes.

A R M A N D M A R S E I L L E D O L L

DATE: *c.*1925 NATIONALITY: **German**
MAKER: **Armand Marseille** MARKS: *370*
HEIGHT: **38cm (15in)**

Armand Marseille's mould number 370 was first used in 1913, and it was one of the company's best known dolls. Like many of the company's moulds, it was used for many years and with a variety of materials. The doll illustrated has a bisque head, with blue sleeping eyes and an open mouth with teeth, and composition body and limbs. The doll is dressed as a Newhaven fisher-girl, in three petticoats (two striped, one flannel), a thick blouse, an apron, knitted wool stockings and a red shawl. (Newhaven, near Edinburgh, was an important fishing port and market.)

KEWPIE DOLL

DATE: *c.*1920 NATIONALITY: **German** MAKER: **Not known**
HEIGHT: **7.5cm (3in)**

Kewpie dolls, which are distinguished by their top-knots of hair, sideways-glancing eyes and all-in-one legs, were originally designed by the artist Rose O'Neill in 1909, and the design was patented *c.*1913. The businessman George Borgfeldt commissioned O'Neill to make the doll, which became one of the two most successful dolls ever made (for the other, Bye-lo Baby, see page 68).

The earliest versions were made by Kestner, but Borgfeldt claimed that by 1914 at least 21 factories were manufacturing Kewpie dolls, including the Cameo Doll Co. of New York City, which made composition versions; Gebrüder Voight, Hermann Voight and other German factories, which made porcelain ones; Karl Standfuss, which made composition ones; and Steiff, which made cloth ones. Kewpie dolls range in size from about 6cm (2½in) to 43cm (17in), and they sometimes have hair, sometimes not; some are black or brown; some have wings; some are undressed, and some, like this one, are dressed in all kinds of uniforms.

UNCLE SAM

DATE: *c.*1896 NATIONALITY: **German**
MAKER: **Cuno & Otto Dressel** HEIGHT: **36cm (14in)**

The firm of Cuno & Otto Dressel was founded at Sonneberg in the 1700s, and by the late 19th century it was exporting much of its output to the USA, where one of its most important customers was Butler Brothers, the toy manufacturers and distributors. This figure of Uncle Sam was made in the late 1890s at a time when US patriotism was running high because of the Cuban insurrection against Spanish rule, which was supported by many Americans. It has a bisque swivel head made by Simon & Halbig, glass eyes and a jointed wooden body. The figure is wearing its original blue felt top hat, felt jacket, cotton trousers, vest and a shirt.

BYE-LO BABY

DATE: 1922 NATIONALITY: **German** MAKER: **Not known**
HEIGHT: **33cm (13in)**

In 1922 a US art teacher named Grace Storey Putnam designed and copyrighted the Bye-lo Baby doll for George Borgfeldt. Putnam had searched through numerous hospitals and orphanages before she found a suitable child on which to model the doll. It was made with a bisque flanged head, a fabric body and celluloid hands. It was an immediate best-seller and enjoyed such huge sales that it is sometimes known as the Million Dollar Baby. Many of the heads were made for Borgfeldt by Alt, Beck & Gottschalck of Nauendorf, but Borgfeldt also ordered heads from, among others, Hertel, Schwab & Co. of Stutzhaus, Kestner of Waltershausen and Karl Standfuss of Dresden, and from the Cameo Doll Co. and Louis Sametz, both of New York. The doll was made in several sizes, including the small all-bisque one seen here.

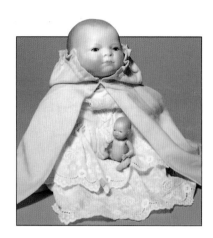

NOBBI KID

DATE: **1920s** NATIONALITY: **German** MARKS: *A 253 M Nobbi Kid Reg. US Pat. Germany 11/10* HEIGHT: **18cm (7in)**

This bisque-headed doll, with a closed mouth and googly eyes, has a composition toddler-type body. The dress is original to the doll, but the real hair wig is a later addition. Nobbi Kid was one of the dolls commissioned by George Borgfeldt, and the design was registered in 1915. This version was made by Armand Marseille, which registered its own mould number, 253, for the design in 1925.

DPC DOLL

DATE: **1908** NATIONALITY: **English** MAKER: **DPC**
MARKS: *Hanley, England* HEIGHT: **43cm (17in)**

There is some confusion about the identity of the company represented by the initials DPC. A doll so marked could be made by the Diamond Pottery Co. or by the Doll Pottery Co., both of which were operating at about the same time and in the same area of Staffordshire in the UK. However, this doll, which has a bisque head and composition body, is marked *Hanley, England*, and because the Diamond Pottery Co. was situated in Shelton, on the outskirts of Hanley, and the Doll Pottery Co. in Fenton, Staffordshire, it seems reasonable to assume that the former firm made it.

GOSS DOLL

DATE: *c.*1918 NATIONALITY: **English**
MAKER: **W.H. Goss & Co.** HEIGHT: **38cm (15in)**

The Staffordshire firm of W.H. Goss & Co. made porcelain busts during the 19th century, and during the first few decades of the 20th century it made fine bisque heads, supplying the English market during World War I, when German dolls were not available. It also produced baby dolls during World War II. The company's dolls have glass eyes and are rather heavily painted, compared with German and French dolls of the same period. The red lips and heavy eyebrows of this doll are typical of Goss bisque dolls, which are quite rare. The doll has a bisque head and shoulder-plate, fixed eyes and a crude cloth body.

GILLIE CHARLSON DOLL

DATE: **1986** NATIONALITY: **English**
MAKER: **Gillie Charlson** HEIGHT: **46cm (18in)**

English doll-maker Gillie Charlson created 17 oriental dolls in 1986 for the movie *Shanghai Surprise* starring Madonna. She had to make the dolls in only five weeks. She used an oriental head mould and wired porcelain arms to the body, which was simply a wooden frame on a wooden base, padded to give it shape. The "embroidered" robe was actually painted with textured paint, and it hides the fact that the doll has no legs.

SOPHY

DATE: **1990s** NATIONALITY: **English** MAKER: **Lynne and Michael Roche**
HEIGHT: **58.5cm (23in)**

After a period of making reproduction antique dolls, the first "modern" doll that Lynne and Michael Roche of Bath, UK, made was based on a photograph of the French writer Colette as a child. That was in 1982, and since then they have made many other fine models with bisque heads and bodies. Recently they have used jointed wooden bodies. All the dolls are marked on the head and on the body with the copyright date, the name of the doll, its number and the names of the makers. This doll, Sophy, is made in several sizes, including an all-bisque 30cm (12in) version. The size seen here is in a limited edition of 100. It has a ball-jointed wooden body and porcelain hands.

ROYAL CHILDREN

DATE: *c.*1953 NATIONALITY: **American**
MAKER: **Martha Thompson** HEIGHT: **24cm (9½in)**

The late Martha Thompson's dolls were inspired by
literary and historical events. She was fascinated by
the British royal family and made a set of dolls
representing Prince Charles at four different stages in
his childhood. The dolls are in flesh-coloured bisque.
These two, representing Prince Charles and Princess
Anne, have cloth bodies and bisque lower limbs.
They were made in honour of the Queen's coronation
in 1953. Among Martha Thompson's other portrait
dolls are Mamie and Dwight Eisenhower, Princess
Grace and Prince Rainier of Monaco, Princess
Margaret and Jacqueline Onassis.

JOHN WAYNE

DATE: *c.*1970 NATIONALITY: **American** MAKER: **Effanbee**
HEIGHT: **40cm (16in)**

Although the most collectable of the Effanbee dolls
are those made before World War II (see page 44),
the company has continued to manufacture a range
of dolls, which will doubtless be among the
collectibles of the future. Both these John Wayne
dolls have bisque heads. The doll on the left has
moulded blue eyes, eyelashes, eyebrows and hair
and a cloth body. It is dressed in the uniform of a
cavalry officer. The right-hand doll, which also has a
cloth body, is dressed in a cowboy outfit.

CELLULOID, PLASTIC AND VINYL DOLLS

PETITCOLIN DOLL

DATE: *c.*1920 NATIONALITY: **French** MAKER: **Petitcolin**
MARKS: ***Tête de l'aigle France 57½*** HEIGHT: **52cm (20½in)**

This French all-celluloid doll has the eagle head (*tête de l'aigle*) mark of Petitcolin of Paris, which was established in 1914. The firm's registered trademark was the side view of an eagle's head. The dolls' hands are particularly well modelled, and the moulded hair-style dates the doll to the 1920s.

SNF CHARACTER DOLL

DATE: *c.*1927 NATIONALITY: **French** MAKER: **SNF**
HEIGHT: **43cm (17in)**

The celluloid character doll has moulded bobbed hair, fixed glass eyes with lashes, a celluloid body and limbs, jointed shoulders and hips and a swivel neck. The initials SNF stand for Société Nobel Française, about which little is known although its mark is one of the most often found on French celluloid dolls of this period. The Société Industrielle de Celluloid began to make celluloid dolls in Paris in about 1902. It used a material called Sicoid or Sicoïne, a pyroxylin material, and its mark was the winged dragon or wyvern with a shield. It merged with the manufacturing firm of Neumann & Marx (the initials *N&M* appear in the shield), and its successor was SNF, which continued to use the earlier trademark until 1939, when the mark *SNF* within a diamond was registered. The doll is wearing its original red flannel dress under a white pinafore decorated with drawings of children playing. Underneath are a tucked and lace-trimmed petticoat, nylon drawers (replacement), white socks and pretty red shoes with rosettes.

KÄMMER & REINHARDT DOLL

DATE: **1910** NATIONALITY: **German** MAKER: **Kämmer & Reinhardt**
MARKS: ***K&R 406/1*** HEIGHT: **40cm (16in)**

Kämmer & Reinhardt was among the many German doll-making companies to make celluloid dolls. This doll, which has a celluloid head and composition body, bears, in addition to the Kämmer & Reinhardt mark, the turtle mark, *Schildkröte*, of the Rheinische Gummi-und Celluloid-Fabrik of Mannheim-Neckarau. This company, which was founded in 1873 and was initially a factory producing rubber goods, became the primary German producer of celluloid dolls, supplying heads and doll parts to many other manufacturers, including Kämmer & Reinhardt, which it was supplying with celluloid heads as early as 1902. Its trademark is, therefore, often found in combination with another maker's mark. This doll has sleeping eyes, an open mouth, a swivel head and a jointed composition body. The doll, which has its original hair, is wearing a bridesmaid's dress.

KESTNER CHARACTER DOLL

DATE: **early 20th century** NATIONALITY: **German**
MAKER: **J.D. Kestner** MARKS: ***K*** HEIGHT: **36cm (14in)**

This Kestner all-celluloid doll bears the initial *K* of the Waltershausen doll-makers, but it is more than likely that the head was supplied by Rheinische Gummi-und Celluloid-Fabrik, which probably used one of Kestner's own moulds. Kestner claimed, in fact, that its celluloid dolls were matt-finished and that the colours would not fade in the sun. However, given the source of the head, there can have been little difference between the quality of the material of Kestner's dolls and the majority of celluloid dolls being produced in Germany at this period. The colours of this bent-limbed character baby have certainly faded somewhat.

MINERVA HEAD

DATE: **early 20th century** NATIONALITY: **German**
MAKER: **Buschow & Beck** MARKS: *Minerva*
HEIGHT: **10cm (4in)**

Minerva metal heads on shoulder-plates such as this one are most often found in the UK. Buschow & Beck of Reichenbach was known chiefly for metal heads, but it also manufactured celluloid heads. The name Minerva was registered in 1894, and from about 1900 the heads were made of brass – these are very collectable – but after about 1907 the brass was replaced by a combination of enamel and celluloid in an attempt to overcome the problems of flaking and chipping inherent with the metal, and this is the material illustrated here. The head has fixed eyes, and the rest of the body would probably have been of celluloid. The embossed name *Minerva* usually appears on the front of the shoulder-plate, while the word *Germany* appears on the back, making identification fairly straightforward.

The New York company Alfred Vischer & Co. was importer and agent for Buschow & Beck, and Vischer registered the name Minerva as a trademark for the metal heads, which it also made, in 1901.

BRITISH NATIONAL DOLL CO. DOLL

DATE: **1950** NATIONALITY: **English**
MAKER: **British National Doll Co.**
MARKS: *BND London* HEIGHT: **25cm (10in)**

The British National Doll Co. was making dolls with china heads in 1933. In 1942 it claimed to be the first UK company to mass-produce composition dolls, and by 1950 it was making hard plastic dolls, such as this one, which is wearing its original romper suit. The doll has sleeping eyes, an open-closed mouth, bent limbs and moulded hair. It is jointed at hips, shoulder and wrists, and it has a swivel neck. The mould line is clearly visible down the sides of the legs. These dolls are generally marked on the nape of the neck.

PEDIGREE DOLLS

DATE: **1948–1950s** NATIONALITY: **English**
MAKER: **Pedigree** HEIGHT: **left-hand doll 61cm**
(24in); right-hand doll 33cm (13in)

The left-hand doll has flirty, sleeping eyes,
moulded curly hair, a swivel head, bent arms
that are jointed at the shoulders, and slightly
bent legs that are jointed at the hips. This is a
"talking" doll, with a voice box at the back. The
right-hand doll, although smaller, is similar in
many respects but the colours have faded more.
(See also page 45.)

KEWPIE DOLL

DATE: **1970s** NATIONALITY: **English** MAKER: **Not known**
HEIGHT: **23cm (9in)**

The Kewpie doll has retained its popularity to the present day since
it was first designed by Rose O'Neill before World War II. It is
interesting to compare this vinyl version with the 1920s bisque
doll on page 67. This doll has the same top-knot of hair, sideways
glance and "starfish" hands, but it has a swivel neck and is
jointed at the shoulders and hips.

MARKS BROTHERS HEAD

DATE: **1918–30** NATIONALITY: **American**
MAKER: **Marks Brothers Co.** MARKS: **6**
HEIGHT: **15cm (6in)**

Marks Brothers Co. was based in Boston, Massachusetts, and it made and imported celluloid socket- and shoulder-heads from 1918 until the late 1920s. Its mark was *Made in USA/Marks Brothers Co. Boston* within a shield, and a number was often placed on the back of the shoulder-head indicating the height of the head in inches. This celluloid head has moulded hair and painted features.

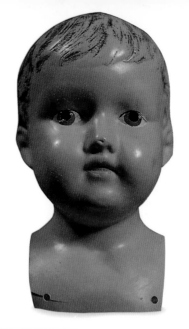

GOODYEAR DOLL

DATE: *c.*1920 NATIONALITY: **American**
MAKER: **Charles Goodyear** HEIGHT: 38cm (15in)

The Goodyear Rubber Co. was among several manufacturers that experimented with making rubber dolls. In theory, rubber was an ideal material for dolls as it was both safe and unbreakable; unfortunately, however, it has not proved to be durable. This rubber baby doll dating from about 1920, for example, has lost almost all of its paint and some of the "skin" surface. It does, however, give a good idea of the rather chunky, square face and chubby neck. The original painted doll would have looked much more attractive. The rubber heads were attached to stuffed cloth bodies.

Rubber dolls made by Goodyear, which was founded in New Haven, Connecticut, are marked *Goodyear* or *Goodyear's Pat. May 6, 1851. Ext 1865*. The year 1851 was when Nelson Goodyear, Charles's brother, patented his invention of hard rubber. The New York Rubber Co. and Benjamin F. Lee made rubber dolls under licence from Goodyear.

MADAME ALEXANDER DOLLS

DATE: **1970s** NATIONALITY: **American** MAKER: **Alexander Doll Co.**
MARKS: **left-hand doll 3** *Alexander 1979* HEIGHT: **left-hand doll 38cm (15in)**

The Alexander Doll Co. of New York was founded by Madame Alexander in 1923, and the dolls made by Beatrice Alexander Behrman and by the company she founded are among the best loved of all American collectors' dolls. They are seldom found in Europe. The early dolls produced by the company were made of cloth, but it has made dolls in almost every new material since then. The two dolls illustrated here have vinyl heads and limbs, stuffed soft bodies, rooted hair and sleeping eyes. Both dolls are wearing their original clothes.

The left-hand doll is to a design known as Little Brother; there are also dolls known as Little Sister. The right-hand doll, which is known as Baby Precious, is a 1974 model. One of the major problems of identifying Madame Alexander dolls is the fact that many of the early dolls had only a paper label attached to the wrist or a label stitched onto the clothes.

GENERAL MILLS DOLL

DATE: **1970** NATIONALITY: **American**
MAKER: **General Mills** HEIGHT: **48cm (19in)**

This doll with its vinyl head and hard plastic body was made by the US manufacturer General Mills. It has sleeping eyes, an open-closed mouth, jointed hips and shoulders and a swivel neck. There are also joints at the wrists and waist, so that when the battery-operated mechanism is activated by a string, the doll bows and turns from the waist.

GLOSSARY

· · · · · · · · · · · · ·

applied ears Ears that have been applied to the head after it has been moulded, as opposed to ears that are an integral part of the head.

armature An internal framework, usually metal, used to give shape and form to cloth, leather and papier mâché bodies.

bébé A doll that has the proportions of a young child and a shorter, fatter body than a lady doll.

bisque Also sometimes called biscuit, a ceramic material that can be poured into a mould or pressed into shape before being fired at high temperature. Bisque dolls' heads were often painted before being fired for a second time at a lower temperature. Bisque has a matt, unglazed surface.

bonnet-head A doll with a hat or bonnet moulded as an integral part of the head.

breveté or **bte** The French term, sometimes incised on dolls' heads or bodies, indicating that a design has been patented.

carton Cardboard.

celluloid A material used for dolls between about 1890 and 1940. First developed by the Hyatt Brothers of New Jersey, this was used in much the same way as bisque. It was superseded by more stable and less inflammable vinyls and plastics.

china-head A doll with a head of glazed porcelain, a ceramic material that was widely used for dolls' heads before being superseded by bisque in the second half of the 19th century.

composition A word used for several substances, including papier mâché, which were used to make dolls' bodies and heads. It was usually made of wood pulp and an adhesive, mixed together with colouring agents.

deponiert See *déposé.*

déposé The French word, sometimes found incised in a doll's bisque shoulder-plate or head, indicating that an application for a patent had been registered. Like the German equivalent, *deponiert*, it was often shortened to *dep.*

DRGM (*Deutsches Reichsgebrauchsmuster*) These initials, used in Germany after 1909, indicate that a design or patent has been registered.

DRMR (*Deutsches Reichsmusterrolle*) These initials on a doll indicate that the patent application has been entered on the German government roll of design patents.

DRP (*Deutsches Reichspatent*) The initials were used on German dolls to indicate that a government patent had been granted.

fixed neck A head mounting in which there is no joint between the head and the shoulder-plate, which were made in one piece.

ges. gesch. The abbreviation, standing for *Gesetzlich geschützt*, found on both dolls' heads and dolls' bodies made by German producers and used to indicate that patent rights had been registered and granted.

g.m. The abbreviation, standing for *Geschmacksmuster*, found on German dolls' heads and bodies, indicates that a design patent has been registered and that a design must not be copied by a third party.

papier mâché A paper pulp, combined with a whitening agent and a suitable glue, that was used for the manufacture of dolls' heads and bodies in the early 19th century. Towards the end of the 19th century a type of papier mâché was developed that could be poured into a mould rather than having to be pressure-moulded; it was both stronger and more durable than the earlier mixture.

Parian True Parian (i.e., marble from Paros) was not used for dolls, but imitation Parian, a pure white, fine porcelain, was sometimes used for dolls' heads. The features were generally painted, although glass eyes were occasionally inserted.

pat or **patd** The abbreviation used on US and UK dolls to indicate that a design had been patented.

pate Dolls' heads were sometimes made with a hole in the crown through which the maker could insert the eyes or complete stringing. This hole was covered by a papier mâché or composition pad or pate, which was shaped to follow the curve of the head and which provided a firm base for attaching a wig.

poured wax The type of doll's head and limbs created by pouring molten wax into a mould so that the wax that is in contact with the mould cools and hardens while the remaining, still molten wax is poured away. Such dolls are extremely fragile.

pumpkin-head A style of doll's head characterized by a broad face and a certain lack of depth from front to back.

SFBJ (*Société Française de Fabrication de Bébés et Jouets*) A syndicate of French doll manufacturers, founded in 1899 by, among others, Bru, Fleischmann & Bloedel, Gaultier, Genty, Girard, Gobert, Jumeau, Pintel & Godchaux, Rabery & Delphieu and Remignard, to counter the threat posed by German manufacturers. Later, A. Bouchet, Daniel & Cie and P.H. Schmitz joined.

shoulder-head A doll in which the head and shoulders are moulded in one piece.

slit-head A style of doll's head, common in the mid-19th century, with a slit running from the front to the back of the head into which hair is inserted. This results in the doll appearing to have a central parting, with, often, ringlets falling to each side.

wax-over The expression used to describe dolls that have a core of a material such as papier mâché or composition that is dipped into, or painted with, molten wax.

FURTHER READING

Cieslik, Jürgen and Marianne, *German Doll Encyclopedia 1800– 1939*, Hobby House Press Inc., Maryland, 1985/White Mouse Publications, London, 1985

Coleman, D.S., E.A. and E.J., *The Collector's Encyclopedia of Dolls*, vol i, Robert Hale, London, 1970/Crown Publishers Inc., New York, 1968; vol ii, Robert Hale, London, 1987/Crown Publishers Inc., New York, 1986

Earnshaw, Nora, *Collecting Dolls*, Collins, London, 1987

Foulke, Jan, *Kestner: King of Dollmakers*, Hobby House Press Inc., Maryland, 1982

Foulke, Jan, *Simon & Halbig Dolls: The Artful Aspect*, Hobby House Press Inc., Maryland, 1984

Gerwat-Clark, Brenda, *The Collector's Book of Dolls*, Apple Press, London, 1987

Goodfellow, Caroline G., *Understanding Dolls*, Antique Collectors' Club, Woodbridge, Suffolk, 1983

Hillier, Mary, *The History of Wax Dolls*, Souvenir Press, London, 1985/Hobby House Press Inc., Maryland, 1985

Jackson Douet, Valerie, *World Guide to Dolls*, Apple Press, London, 1993

King, Constance Eileen, *A Collector's History of Dolls*, Robert Hale, London 1977

King, Constance Eileen, *Jumeau: Prince of Dollmakers*, Hobby House Press Inc., Maryland 1983

Seeley, M. and V., *How to Collect French Bébé Dolls*, HP Books, Tucson, Arizona, 1985

Tarnowska, Maree, *Fashion Dolls*, Souvenir Press, London, 1986/ Hobby House Press Inc., Maryland, 1986

Tarnowska, Maree, *Rare Character Dolls*, Souvenir Press, London, 1987/Hobby House Press Inc., Maryland, 1987

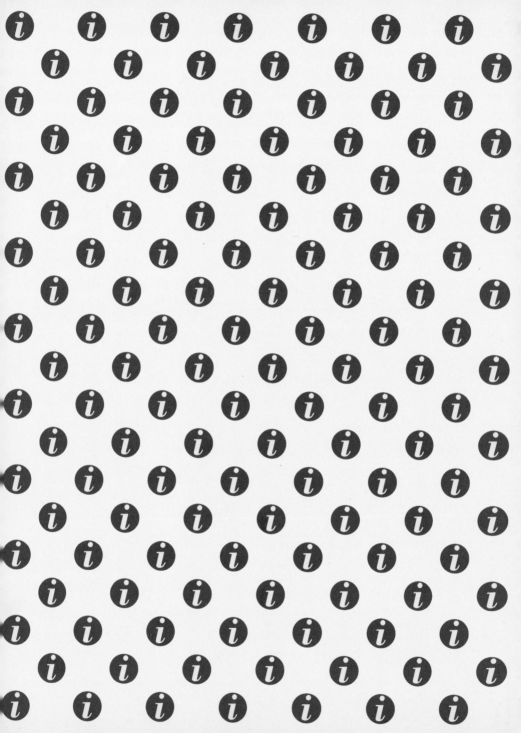